Faith, Forensics, and Firearms

A Spiritual Psychoanalysis of Three Forensic Trauma Cases

Charles Zeiders, PsyD

CHIRON PUBLICATIONS • ASHEVILLE, NORTH CAROLINA

www.ChironPublications.com

Interior and cover design by Danijela Mijailovic
Printed primarily in the United States of America.

ISBN 978-1-63051-664-2 paperback
ISBN 978-1-63051-665-9 hardcover
ISBN 978-1-63051-666-6 electronic
ISBN 978-1-63051-667-3 limited edition paperback

"Keeping Christ in Counseling: Recent and Developing Threats Eroding Precious Rights to Religious Freedom and Client Self-Determination," from *Transformative Encounters: The Intervention of God in Christian Counseling and Pastoral Care*, by David W. Appleby. Reproduced with permission of IVP Academic in the format Republish in a book via Copyright Clearance Center.

"An Interview with Noam Chomsky," by Nicholas Haggerty, April 9, 2015, from *Commonweal Magazine*. Copyright © 2015 Commonweal Foundation, reprinted with permission, www.commonwealmagazine.org.

"5 Quotes from Pope Francis on Racism, Xenophobia and Immigration" by Nadra Kareem Nittle, May 15, 2017, https://www.thoughtco.com. Used by permission of Dotdash.

Library of Congress Cataloging-in-Publication Data

Names: Zeiders, Charles, author.
Title: Faith, forensics, and firearms : a spiritual psychoanalysis of three forensic
    trauma cases / Charles Zeiders.
Description: Asheville, N.C.: Chiron Publications, [2018] | Includes biblio-
    graphical references and index.
Identifiers: LCCN 2018041710| ISBN 9781630516642 (pbk. : alk. paper) | ISBN
    9781630516659 (hardcover : alk. paper)
Subjects: LCSH: Psychic trauma--Treatment--Case studies. | Forensic
    psychology--Case studies. | Psychology--Religious aspects--Christianity--
    Case studies.
Classification: LCC RC552.T7 Z45 2018 | DDC 616.85/21--dc23
LC record available at https://lccn.loc.gov/2018041710

Books by the Same Author

- *The Clinical Christ:*
  Scientific and Spiritual Reflections on the Tranformative Psychology
  Called Christian Holism

- *Love Poems and Other Terrible Problems*

- *Wall Street Revolution and Other Poems*

Contents

Foreword, by Douglas Schoeninger   7

A Word About Forensic Psychology   9

Introduction   11

    1. Faith, Forensics, and Firearms   17

    2. A Plight Like Job's: Trauma, Grief, and Betrayal   45

    3. The Citizen Who Sued the Police and the Political

       Spiritualties of Otherness   81

Afterword, by Dale Michaels   109

Acknowledgments   115

About the Author   116

About the Contributors   117

Sources   118

Dedication

To the woman in the dead city
To the man at cliff's edge
To the one who weeps without hope of comfort.

Foreword

By Douglas Schoeninger

To have your day in court requires that someone cares to hear you, honor the sacredness of your experience, and help you articulate what's happened to you and those close to you who have also been impacted.

A forensic evaluator is charged with assessing the facts—what happened, the impact of what happened, and the psychological condition of the person(s) as a consequence of events and in relation to how events were perceived and are remembered. Standing before the forensic evaluator is a child of God, one who has been deeply wounded and is faced with re-traumatization through the process of litigation. The evaluator is challenged with the tasks of objective assessment and at the same time, providing a safe and caring presence that makes honest disclosure possible. While forensic evaluation is an assessment and not a therapeutic intervention, the evaluator does well to be cognizant of how the encounter impacts the person's sense of being fairly considered and fairly heard, and in this sense is part of the person's healing process.

A fair hearing also requires consideration of the examinee's family context and loyalties, psychological makeup, the wounding impact of the events, and possible distortions of perception, memory, and imagination by those who allegedly have perpetrated violence and trauma.

As Dr. Zeiders sensitively illustrates, such listening is best done with an attunement to the Holy Spirit, who is present and available assisting objectivity with love and providing potentially healing touch through the encounter. Charles understands that the forensic evaluative encounter requires both objectivity and care for the person, and that these are not in conflict. While he is doing science, he understands that the way he listens and allows the sacred uniqueness of the person to register in his soul has a potentially healing impact. Justice and healing are the context of his approach. He believes that God is working redemptively to turn all things to the good on all sides, and the forensic encounter is part of that process.

Each of the cases presented in this book is followed by a reflective interview, as I address questions to Charles and he elaborates his thoughts from both Jungian-psychological and Christian-theological viewpoints, and applies these insights to the societal context in which the events took place. These dialogic reflections make this work especially valuable for both depth psychologists and theologians, and for all in the legal system— attorneys, judges, paralegals, etc. Charles' words and phrasing are exceptionally creative and incisive, and he shares his rich and enriching inner dialogue to help us integrate perspectives. As he gives voice to his Jungian and Christian insights, each adds dimensionality to the other.

From a Jungian perspective, Charles sees the potential for the crisis of the forensic experience to call forth the God archetype within the plaintiff, supporting the person's process of individuation. In alchemical terms, the plaintiff experiences the base metal of his/her psyche begin to transform into the precious gold of their unique personhood. As a forensic examiner, Charless is witness to this potential and the imprint of the unique soul before him.

From a Christian perspective, Charles sees a sacred soul made in the image of God suffering a crisis inflicted by the traumatic events and litigation, at the same time sustained by the presence of the Holy Spirit and the indwelling of God's healing love. Herein is the potential not only to survive the trauma of litigation, but to heal and grow in manifesting the unique image of God (precious gold) that is this person. Experiencing the power of resurrection through trauma and recovery, the litigant is able to awaken his/her true self, made in the image of God, providing a spiritual foundation for the individuation of the psyche Jung describes.

Charles embeds all of this reflection and analysis in the current cultural context of the United States, speaking to the ravages of prejudicial objectification of people, the exclusion of *others* who are not *us*. In Jungian terms, we project our shadow onto others, the *not-us*, leading to the fracturing of human community, which is meant to be a whole of unique persons and cultures learning from and honoring the image of God in each other and finding our way to a genuinely beneficial mutuality.

A Word About Forensic Psychology

Forensic psychology lies at the intersection between psychology and the justice system. It requires a fundamental understanding of judicial principles and the ability to reformulate psychological findings into legal language for the court. In some cases, a forensic evaluation is ordered to assess the state of mind of the defendant. This evaluation might include a person's history of mental illness, substance abuse, personality assessment, socioeconomic status, and family relations, as these bear on the case.

Introduction

"In dealing with darkness you have to cling to the Good,
otherwise the devil devours you."
— C.G. Jung[1]

"For the plaintiff, winning or losing a lawsuit is purgatorial moment."
— A forensic psychologist

"Mercy triumphs over judgment."
— James 2:13

"Come unto me, all ye that travail are heavy laden, and I will refresh you."
— Jesus Christ, in Matthew 11:28

"Man...is branded by the stain of separation from God. This state of things
would be insupportable if there were nothing to set against evil but the
law...as in pre-Christian [times]—until the reformer and rabbi Jesus tried
to introduce the...advanced and psychologically... correct view that not
fidelity to the law but love and kindness are the antithesis of evil."
— C.G. Jung[2]

---

[1] Ann Conrad Lammers and Adrian Cunningham, eds., *The Jung-White Letters* (New York: Routledge, 2007), 219.

[2] C. G. Jung, *Mysterium Coniunctionis: An Inquiry into the Separation and Synthesis of Psychic Opposites in Alchemy.* Collected Works Vol. 14 (Princeton: Princeton University Press, 1977), 206.

Our sense of justice lies deep within. If we cannot access it directly, our religious imagination will manufacture it, and it will become an impeding apocalypse, or a wish-fulfillment fantasy. When the Ghibelline party exiled Dante from his beloved Florence in 1302, he quite literally found a place for them in hell, marinating them eternally in sewage, boiling them in rivers of blood—and otherwise torturing the traumatizers of his joy. Despite this dark justice, the plaintiff poet journeyed long through the rest of hell and all of purgatory, before obtaining the graceful restitutions of paradise. Dante's experience is universal: The infliction of unjust trauma thrusts us into an "in-between state," liminality, limbo—the consciousness of normality wrecked without an obvious replacement.

In modern times, before, during, and after the hell of a lawsuit and its frequently disorienting conclusion, the plaintiff suffers. And suffers. If the court finally awards cash, the money may fail to heal the traumatized soul. If the suit is lost, disappointment, salted with re-traumatization from humiliating cross-examinations, may leave the litigant's second condition worse than the first. Anything can happen in court.

Seeking civil redress for trauma, the plaintiff understandably resorts to a lawsuit. The justice system, they assume, has the power to repair the plaintiff's life through its archetypal role: to balance the scales of justice in proportion to the wrong.[3] But a favorable outcome may restore the plaintiff's soul no more than an unfavorable one. Something about the process is insufficient. Neither the system nor the ruling can bless away the bleeding portion of the traumatized heart. The gavel comes down. The plaintiff is victorious. Or vanquished. In either case, the attorney must be paid. Yet, the plaintiff has still been raped, beaten, humiliated, violated, and treated unjustly (they allege); and all this has happened in a moment of unrecoverable time, no matter the outcome.

What does this have to do with the forensic case studies and follow-up discussions in this book? Two things. First, I want to demonstrate how the forensic psychologist renders the condition of these traumata for the

---

[3] "Aquinas (d. 1274) developed his theory of justice by drawing directly from Aristotle (d. 322 BC) … [T]he clear link between Aristotle and Aquinas is the basic understanding of justice as *suum cuique* (Lat.), giving each his due…" Richard P. McBrien, *The HarperCollins Encyclopedia of Catholicism* (San Francisco: HarperSanFrancisco: 1995), 1203.

courts; in the role of expert and with the diligence with which Dante explored heaven and hell, the forensic psychologist examines the plaintiff and answers the referral questions put forth by the legal authorities. In the role of scientist, the psychologist establishes the objective merits of the case using the standardized methods of social science (i.e. diagnostic interviewing, psychometric testing, and so forth). Then the examiner writes a report for which he accounts under oath—during deposition, in court, or both. Second, and less obvious, the depth-minded psycho-therapist might consider the spiritual problematics of the forensic situation. What transpersonal or spiritual psychology informs the case? How might spirituality help the plaintiff heal from the primary trauma that brings them to court? How might interacting with God contribute to the plaintiff's positive exit from the purgatories of court and the lawsuit's aftermath? The first concern is that of the forensic expert, the second that of a healer.

This book addresses both, focusing particularly on the second. With my interlocutor, Dr. Douglas Schoeninger, past president of the Association of Christian Therapists and editor of the *Journal of Christian Healing*, I interrogate three cases. For each, I offer the forensic report (with permission of the plaintiffs and their attorneys) for which the plaintiffs retained me to render findings. Then, using these blinded reports as points of departure, Dr. Schoeninger and I discuss the potential transpersonal dimensions of the cases in terms of depth psychology. To address the spiritual, I employ Christian thoughts and symbols, because, as a practicing Anglican, this is the spiritual arena in which I am most familiar. But, whereas my goal is to make a social-scientific statement rather than a pious one, I contextualize these spiritual speculations within the Jungian framework that informs the bulk of my psychotherapeutic work.

I often refer to Roman Catholic spirituality, theology, and doctrine, as well. For the Western world, the Roman Catholic Church—despite its well-publicized imperfections—may be the last institution to link the value of the individual to the heart of a God who loves them limitlessly. Clinical experience teaches that the collision of the broken heart with the Sacred Heart results in surprising psychic healing. In my psychotherapies with very religious patients, I witness clinical states of transformative grace, and I have no doubt that such phenomena are available to many traumatized plaintiffs. Civil society and its jurisprudence would do well to remain mindful that the citizen and sojourner is valuable to God—the Deity who commands a posture of kindness toward them—even if we think the *other* (or *Other*) is wrong—as we share our lives within the crowded polis. Jung certainly thought these religious ideas were worth preserving.[4,5]

> At a time when a large part of mankind is beginning to discard Christianity, it may be worth our while to try to understand why it was accepted in the first place. It was accepted as a means of escape from the brutality and unconsciousness in the ancient world. As soon as we discard it, the old brutality returns in force...[6]

What especially interests me is how such spirituality may advance the healing of the plaintiff's trauma in a manner that is scientifically relevant to the case; how intact faith might ameliorate soul-level agonies from the trauma of sudden, catastrophic, irreversible loss; and how in the face of unjust justice, a plaintiff might maintain a spiritually derived self-image that diminishes the injustice of trauma and the trauma of injustice.

Finally, it seems to me that the trauma of trauma, the trauma of litigation, and the trauma of the aftermath land the plaintiff in what Jungian analyst Lionel Corbett describes as a liminal period, a period of transition when trauma and trial open the plaintiff's soul to the possibility of depth transformation.

---

[4] Jung's contemporary, the Anglo-Catholic poet T.S. Eliot, shared this concern. "I do not believe that the culture of Europe could survive the complete disappearance of the Christian Faith... If Christianity goes, the whole culture goes." T.S. Eliot, *Notes Towards the Definition of Culture* (London: Faber and Faber, 1973), 122.

[5] The conditions of postmodernism may inhibit the spontaneous availability of restorative religious imagery within the collective unconscious (or Objective Psyche). "It becomes harder and harder to live out a life within the premodern condition of an undisturbed traditional society or even within the modern condition of a strong and well-organized belief system. All the major-league belief systems are still around, but all of them are in some kind of postmodern trouble...We are living in a new world, a world that does not know how to define itself...". Walt Anderson, *The Truth about the Truth: De-confusing and Re-constructing the Postmodern World* (New York: TarcherPerigee, 1995), 6.

[6] Edward Hoffman, ed., *The Wisdom of Carl Jung* (New York: Citadel Press, 2003), 163.

The descent into liminality can be seen from either a spiritual or a purely secular point of view. If the psychotherapist is interested in the spiritual dimensions of psychotherapy, this period can be seen as motivated by the transpersonal Self, as part of the necessary destiny of the individual, part of a spiritual or archetypal process such as the dark night of the soul described by John of the Cross. The psychotherapist then has to bear in mind that initiation into a new consciousness often requires both suffering and patient submission to powers higher than oneself. Indeed, the spiritually-oriented therapist may see suffering as one of the ways that the transpersonal dimension claims our attention. This provides another perspective on suffering beside the everyday egoic perspective.[7]

My hope in offering these forensic case studies, replete with the spiritually oriented conversations that follow each, is to stimulate a greater appreciation for the dimensional spiritual resources that are available for society's trauma survivors. For the plaintiff's soul, the profound limitations of secular justice may be offset by the experience of divine blessing.

---

[7] Lionel Corbett, *The Soul in Anguish: Psychotherapeutic Approaches to Suffering* (Asheville, NC: Chiron Publications, 2015), 282-283.

CHAPTER ONE

Faith, Forensics, and Firearms

Years after he had endured involuntary hospitalization, Otto De Gaulle (a pseudonym, like all names in these forensic case studies except my own), petitioned the courts to restore his firearms privileges. This chapter (like the two case studies that follow) is divided into three sections: The first introduces the case and describes how ethics were a primary consideration for me in assuming the assignment. It also describes the unfolding of the proceedings. Critical to the legal determination was the documented impact of the citizen's experience as a practicing Christian, embedded in other health and safety considerations. Section Two provides a blinded rendition (i.e., identifying information has been changed) of the forensic report, which demonstrated that the citizen was mentally fit to carry arms safely. Section Three is a brief interview with the author by Douglas Schoeninger, exploring professional and spiritual issues surrounding forensic practice and the considerations of the depth psychologist.

Introduction

When I was a graduate student at Immaculata University, my ethics professor lectured our class of psychology doctoral students that when our professional formation was complete, when we were licensed, clinically skilled, and seasoned, we had an obligation to society to conduct at least some forensic work. Forensic psychology involves the study of human behavior as it applies to the law and can be used to assess individuals within a legal context. She asserted that, like it or not, experienced psychologists blossom into experts and that professional citizenship obligates the psychologist to provide that expertise to the legal system for the good of society. With that lecture in mind, I accepted one of the most onerous cases of my career.

Out of the blue, I received a phone call from a well-spoken man who identified himself as Christian and a graduate student. The man, Otto De Gaulle, told me that he studied environmental science and hoped to conduct research in remote wilderness areas. Because such research involves the threat of attack by wild animals, his safety depended on his ability to carry firearms. This sounded reasonable enough, but the Commonwealth of Pennsylvania, he told me, had withdrawn his legal right to carry or possess firearms.

Years earlier, he had been subjected to involuntary psychiatric hospitalization, which by law, limited his weapons' rights. The Commonwealth was willing to consider restoring his weapons rights, but the stipulations were formidable. A thorough evaluation had to be conducted by a qualified psychologist and that dangerousness and significant psychopathology had to be ruled out with a reasonable degree of certainty, and the forensic examiner had to defend these findings under oath. The report and clean bill of psychological health was integral to the legal process of restoring his access to firearms.

I asked why he had called me, and he admitted that in the wake of several horrific massacres nationwide involving mentally disturbed shooters, his attorney had been unable to find another psychologist who would take the case. Mr. De Gaulle then told me he'd said a simple prayer to the Holy Trinity that he would find an examiner. Then he searched online for psychologists who had some sort of Christian affiliation and solid forensic credentials, and my practice popped up on the short list. "Will you take the case?" he asked. As a practicing Anglo-Catholic, I felt glad that Otto had faith that he had been led to the "right" examiner, but at the same time I was alarmed that he might conflate our shared religious convictions as somehow guaranteeing the clinical and scientific findings of my report. To allow religious commonality to sway scientific findings in such an important matter of public safety would be both illegal and unethical.

I told him I would take his case on the conditions that he submit to an exhaustive psychological interview, that he take one of the most researched metrics of psychological functioning that exists, that he authorize his attorney to release all relevant documents, that I could interview knowledgeable third parties about his behavior and safety, and that I could extensively interview his family, especially his wife, Collette, who would be present during much of the examination. I told him the findings could not be guaranteed, that he quite possibly could suffer the time and expense of the examination only to find that the outcome disappointed him. I might find him unfit to have his firearms privileges restored. Noting that he was also a scientist, Otto accepted these terms, offering that he would cooperate with the examination process to establish the reasonable psychological certainty that he could, or could not, safely carry firearms—all on the terms of best clinical practices.

Otto's examination was exhaustive. It occupied hours of his personal time and my practice allotments, involving frank interviewing around his intimate life, reviewing reams of documents, interviews with third parties, psychometric assessments, and cross-referencing my emerging clinical opinion with peer-reviewed literature, which my research assistant dug out of the databases of the National Institutes of Health.

What emerged was an objective clinical portrait of a man who years earlier had been extremely distressed regarding his physical and mental health, and whose career and marriage had all but collapsed. This clinical picture also demonstrated that Otto had engaged in healing processes that were utterly holistic, involving mental health interventions, physical health care, family and community support, and a personal religious conversion, sustained by regular religious observance and church participation. As the outcomes below show, peer-reviewed literature supports the notion that spiritual experience and religious affiliation tend to statistically drive health outcomes in the direction of health and safety.

Otto is among the 96 percent of American citizens who believe in God or a higher power. Research into such populations indicates a convincing, health-positive link between subjects' religion and mental health. Psychotherapist, ethicist, and author George Ohlschlager, a certified Christian counselor and mediator, writes:

> [Studies establish that] myriad positive correlations shown by literally thousands of empirical studies on the relationship of religion to mental health. This evidence directly counters the long-held bias against religion by many of the leading lights of psychotherapy, who held that religion was inherently

pathological and superstitious, with terrible consequences to persons and society. Searching all the scientific studies of the nineteenth, twentieth and twenty-first centuries, empirical evidence was gathered from nearly three thousand studies that showed that good and healthy religion influenced these various human conditions and relationships:

1. Greater overall well-being – 80 out of 100 studies

2. Greater hope and optimism – 80% of studies found

3. Greater purpose and meaning in life – 15 of 16 studies

4. Greater self-esteem – 16 of 29 studies, or 55%

5. Better adaptation to bereavement – 8 of 17 studies

6. Greater social support – 19 of 20 studies

7. Lower rates of depression – 60 of 93 studies, or 65%

8. Fewer suicides – 57 of 68 studies

9. Less anxiety – 80% of cohort studies, and 86% of clinical trials

10. Less alcohol and drug abuse – 76 of 86 studies, 88%

11. Less delinquency and crime – 28 of 36 studies, or 78%

12. Greater marital happiness and stability – 35 of 38 studies, or 92%.[8]

Otto's health trajectory was certainly in concert with the trend of these findings. My examination determined that the sum of Otto's religious experience, embedded in multiple healing and accountability processes, had resulted in a man whose life since his involuntary hospitalization had transformed into a soundly healthy person with a promising future. He was negative for psychopathology. The preponderance of evidence spoke not only to his sanity but also to his carefulness and safety. There was once clinical reason to suspect he might be unsafe to carry firearms. But now the results contradicted the notion that Otto would be dangerous with

---

[8] George Ohlschlager, "Keeping Christ in Counseling: Recent and Developing Threats Eroding Precious Rights to Religious Freedom and Client Self-Determination," in David W. Appleby and George Ohlschlager (eds.). *Transformative Encounters: The Intervention of God in Christian Counseling and Pastoral Care* (365-381) (Downers Grove, IL: InterVarsity Press, 2013), 370-371.

weapons. I generated the forensic report and forwarded it to Otto's lawyer, Frederick T. A court date was set and arrived quickly.

Courthouse formalities were observed—all rising for the judge, stating the case, and so on. Eventually, I was called to the witness stand. Otto's attorney, the Commonwealth's attorneys, and the judge interrogated me regarding various aspects of the report, the methodologies involved, and the justifications for my findings. All agreed that Otto had participated in the forensic evaluation in good faith. They were also convinced that the exhaustive nature of the forensics had determined within a reasonable degree of psychological certainly that Otto De Gaulle was psychologically healthy and safe to carry firearms. The Commonwealth had no objection to the restoration of firearms to Otto, and the court so ordered it.

When court adjourned, I joined Otto, his wife, Collette, and Frederick T. Fredrick and I both commended the De Gaulles for demonstrating the courage, character, and citizenship to submit to this necessary but intimidating and potentially humiliating state scrutiny. Both Otto and Collette agreed that their personal religious faith and the support of their church family played a sustaining role in weathering the process of firearms restoration—just as it had played a decisive role in their health as a couple.

In the course of that conversation, Otto and I agreed that his forensic report represented an interesting scientific data point regarding the health-positive nature of durable religious observance. Making a formal, objective, and scientific case that his religious behavior increased the probability that he was a safe man was an aspect of the report's credibility in the legal process. Otto demonstrated unusual generosity by offering to release a redacted copy of the report for publication in the *Journal of Christian Healing*. Upon parting, he smiled and reminded me, "I'm a scientist. I know how it is. Important findings have to be published."

What follows is the report approved by him and then a brief interview between the *Journal of Christian Healing* and myself discussing forensic practice and matters of Christian faith as it pertains to depth psychology.

Forensic Psychological Report [blinded]

Client: Otto De Gaulle
Date of evaluation: April 12, 2015
Evaluator: Charles Zeiders, Psy.D., Licensed Psychologist (Pennsylvania)
Date of report: April 26, 2015
Persons present: Otto de Gaulle (client), Collette De Gaulle (wife), and Evaluator

Sources of Information

Documents and Records

- Review of letter from client attorney Frederick T, Esquire to Evaluator, dated 3/27/15
- Review of letter from client attorney Frederick T, Esquire to Pennsylvania State Police Headquarters dated 2/18/15
- Review of electronic correspondence between Frederick T and Daniel X, Assistant Counsel for State Police
- Review of Psychiatric Discharged Summary dictated by Mary Q, M.D., County Community Hospital, dated 11/15/99
- Review of History & Physical Examination dictated by Mary Q, M.D., County Community Hospital, dated 11/11/99
- Review of practice Intake Information form completed by client on 3/26/15
- Review of client's curriculum vitae, last revised 3/15
- Review of Charter University Graduate Transcript, received 3/22/15
- Review of letters of corroboration from third parties:
- Collette De Gaulle (wife) dated 3/25/15 – authenticated via phone 4/9/15
- Burton and Cathy De Gaulle (parents) dated 3/22/15 – authenticated via phone 4/9/15
- Jose V (friend) dated 3/25/15 – authenticated via phone 4/9/15
- Dr. Anthony M (pastor) dated 3/21/15 – authenticated via phone 4/9/15

- Professor Franklin P (academic advisor) dated 4/3/15 – authenticated via phone 4/9/15
- Montgomery C (neighbor and co religionist) dated 4/3/15 – authenticated via phone 4/10/15
- Arthur L, M.D. (primary care physician) dated 4/4/15 – authenticated via phone 4/17/15

Clinical Instruments

Minnesota Multiphasic Personality Inventory-2 (MMPI-2)
Beck Depression Inventory II (BDI-II)
Beck Anxiety Inventory (BAI)

Other

Clinical interview with client Otto De Gaulle (client) and Collette De Gaulle (wife) on 4/12/15, 9:45 am – 3:45 pm.

Reason for Referral and Purpose of Evaluation

Otto De Gaulle sought this psychological evaluation in collaboration with his attorney, Frederick T of Universal Law Offices. Mr. De Gaulle seeks to lawfully possess firearms in the Commonwealth of Pennsylvania. However, in November of 1999, secondary to a marital dispute, Mr. De Gaulle was involuntarily hospitalized and a protection from abuse order was issued against him. Hence, the Commonwealth will not approve Mr. De Gaulle to lawfully possess firearms until Mr. De Gaulle is psychologically evaluated. Correspondence to Mr. T's office from Commonwealth attorneys requires that this evaluation offer:
a) a detailed opinion as to whether Mr. De Gaulle would be a danger to others if he were to possess firearms,
b) and that the evaluation should include any mental health diagnosis/ prognosis that may apply.

Identification

Otto B. De Gaulle is a 43-year-old Caucasian male married to Collette M. De Gaulle. He is employed by Charter University, where he is a graduate student and graduate research assistant in Environmental

Science. His wife, Mrs. De Gaulle, works as an IT supervisor at that same university.

Mr. De Gaulle and his wife have no children but enjoy a close relationship with Mr. De Gaulle's parents, Burton De Gaulle and Cathy De Gaulle of Victory, PA.

Mr. De Gaulle and his wife are active members of Good Samaritan Free Church and have many friends among the congregation.

He and Mrs. De Gaulle reside at [ ].

Presenting Problem

In his Intake Information for this evaluation completed 3/26/15 Mr. De Gaulle identified his presenting problem as follows:

I discovered that a voluntary commitment stemming from an argument with my wife on the phone in November 1999 was coded as an involuntary committal, 302. A 302 excludes me from owning, possessing, and using firearms which are necessary for my line of work. In 2007, I returned to school to get advanced degrees in Environmental Science. In 2012, I discovered the 302 on my record. I may need to carry a firearm for protection from dangerous game in the western US including the states of Montana and Alaska and southern US while conducting research. Some of my research currently is conducted in the Everglades of southern Florida. I have been wading in gator-infested swamps conducting fisheries research with *big gators* (over ten feet) only a few feet away. I also require firearms to safely conduct research in wild areas of the Commonwealth.

On the verge of completing his Master's degree and intending to conduct Doctoral work to pursue a career that involves field research in wild areas of the country, Mr. De Gaulle believes that a firearm would increase his safety when in the field.

During a 4/10/15 phone conversation, Mr. De Gaulle's academic advisor, Franklin P, Professor of Environmental Science, the Professor confirmed that carrying a firearm would increase Mr. De Gaulle's safety. He further noted that firearms are especially welcome "when black bear show up in the field." Professor P also issued a letter that he has confidence in his student's character, mental stability, and capacity to competently handle firearms.

Circumstances of the 302

Two years prior to Mr. De Gaulle's involuntary hospitalization in 1999, Mr. De Gaulle was knocked by a forklift from the portable sawmill that was part of his business at the time. The concussion he sustained left him with health problems and led to financial problems and aggravated marital struggles with sexual adjustment. Health issues included gastrointestinal issues and incontinence. His symptoms of post-concussion syndrome included headache and susceptibility to stress. Stress fueled his GI problems, and just prior to November 1999, Mr. De Gaulle's health further deteriorated from food poisoning that caused an alarming loss of weight—from 190 pounds to 146—in a short span of time.

In poor physical health, exhausted, and worried about money and the durability of his marriage, he and Mrs. De Gaulle began to argue. On the day of the involuntary hospitalization, Mr. De Gaulle reports that he and Mrs. De Gaulle were arguing on the telephone about finances and furniture that they were moving. Mr. De Gaulle was at home. Mrs. De Gaulle was at work. Mr. De Gaulle was upset that Mrs. De Gaulle appeared to undervalue a chest he had given her. In the course of the conversation he angrily kicked and broke a panel of the chest. Contained therein was a gun Mrs. De Gaulle had previously placed there. Mr. De Gaulle admits he "racked the action [a maneuver that prepares the weapon for firing] partly to make sure it was not loaded and partly to scare her." Responding to Mrs. De Gaulle's query about the sound of his handling the weapon, the upset Mr. De Gaulle said, "Do you expect me to blow my head off?" or words to that effect. During the clinical interview, Mr. and Mrs. De Gaulle affirmed that Mr. De Gaulle's behavior represented a maladroit, passion-driven attempt to convey his upset to Mrs. De Gaulle, not a behavior or remark designed to express genuine intent to injure himself or Mrs. De Gaulle.

Responding to pressure from concerned coworkers who were privy to this conversation, Mrs. De Gaulle called the police while Mr. De Gaulle calmed down in the presence of his father. Authorities came to the home and allowed Mr. De Gaulle to be driven to the hospital by his father. Mr. De Gaulle spent 5 days inpatient. In addition to psychiatric care and observation, Mr. De Gaulle received treatment for his gastrointestinal problems. Mr. and Mrs. De Gaulle were under the impression that the inpatient hospitalization was recorded as voluntary. They believe that the 302 status-of-record is possibly a clerical error. Mrs. De Gaulle further noted that she succumbed to pressure from a social worker to sign a PFA against Mr. De Gaulle (Protection from Abuse, a restraining order in Pennsylvania).

In her letter of 3/25/15, Collette De Gaulle elaborates the marital dispute of November, 1999 and notes the following about her impression of Mr. De Gaulle's actual dangerousness with firearms.

> At no time did I have a fear for my well-being. I did not think then or now that Otto would harm me. Soon after the incident I requested the PFA be dropped so Otto and I could attend counseling and move on with our life.

The couple presents a version of the hospitalization wherein Mr. De Gaulle denies the intent to harm and Mrs. De Gaulle denies feeling actually endangered by him. Mr. De Gaulle noted—with Mrs. De Gaulle's agreement—that he also had no real intent to injure himself; he remains embarrassed by the more than decade-old incident.

The couple further agreed that amid the stress and confusion of having various authorities suddenly involved in their marital adjustment issues, they were unable to fully protect their interests or fully appreciate the potential long-term ramifications of the decisions they were making and the papers they were signing. Both noted that they were a younger couple and less mature.

Summary of Previous Psychiatric Findings from Hospitalization

According to reports dictated by Mary Q, MD, Otto De Gaulle was admitted to County Community Hospital on 11/10/99 and discharged on 11/15/99. She describes the patient as a 29-year-old male admitted to the Mental Health Unit on a 302 status. The reason for the referral involved an argument between the couple who had been having sexual and financial difficulties. The couple was in the midst of moving and the patient noticed that his wife was leaving behind a trunk that he had made for her. Reeling from hurt feelings, he destroyed the trunk that led to the escalation and threats of either hurting himself or the wife that led to his being admitted on a 302 basis. Dr. Q noted that there was no previous history of psychiatric treatment, although the patient may have scheduled and then cancelled or missed outpatient mental health evaluations. Prior medical treatment also involved treatment for an inflamed colon with Prednisone, treatment by a neurologist, and a trial of antidepressants for sleep problems and unspecified symptoms. She noted that the patient reported a personal history of sexual abuse perpetrated by a neighbor from age three until nine and also reported problems in school involving shyness and suffering bullying. The history was insignificant for a personal drug or alcohol history.

The course of treatment in the hospital included successfully treating Mr. De Gaulle's stress-related GI problems with steroids. Tests indicated that Mr. De Gaulle's concussion had caused a syndrome known as "post-concussion syndrome," which weakened Mr. De Gaulle's coping capacity in the face of intense stressors. During hospitalization, the patient demonstrated a downcast mood but impressed the psychiatrist as intelligent with appropriate and controlled behavior. Mr. De Gaulle admitted to Dr. Q that he made a statement prior to admission regarding taking a gun and blowing his head off, but Dr. Q also noted that the patient's judgment was largely intact and that he denied suicidal or homicidal ideation or intent. He was discharged without medications and referred to outpatient counseling. Discharge Diagnoses were as follows:

Axis I	Depressive Disorder, Not Otherwise Specified
Axis II	Personality Disorder, Not Otherwise Specified, primary diagnosis
Axis III	Persistent Post-Concussion Syndrome
Axis IV	Moderately severe financial limitations, currently unemployed, and serious marital problems.

Summary of Other Mental Health Treatment History

From the inpatient hospitalization, Mr. De Gaulle was referred to Ivan X of the Center for Psychotherapy, with whom he discussed his concerns and marital adjustment issues. In 2005, the client saw a Dr. Ned E due to a flare-up of marital contention that deteriorated the couple's rapport. (Retrospectively the couple agreed that much of their conflict at the time may have been driven by the interference of a relative who kept advising Mrs. De Gaulle to leave Mr. De Gaulle.) Mr. De Gaulle was looking for guidance due to the fact that Mrs. De Gaulle had filed for divorce. Mr. De

Gaulle did not want the divorce and hoped to avert it. When Dr. Ned E advised Mr. De Gaulle that the only way he could heal was to let the divorce happen, Mr. De Gaulle discontinued treatment with Dr. E and sought the advice of his pastor, Dr. Anthony M, and his best friend Jose V, a church elder. Mr. De Gaulle began to rely on his Christian community and spiritual coping to handle his stress and concerns about his marriage. In 2005, Mrs. De Gaulle agreed to participate in marriage counseling with Gwen J of The Marital Institute. The couple found that the communication skills they gained from this clinician instrumental in helping them communicate in a respectful, attentive fashion, which led to an increase in marital rapport and friendship. Mrs. De Gaulle dropped her plans for divorce.

Spiritual and Religious History and Impressions of Religious Community

Mr. De Gaulle presents as a sincerely practicing Christian. When troubled in his life and marriage, Mr. De Gaulle sought counsel from his friend Jose V, a church elder, and respected Pastor Dr. Anthony M. In 2005 Mr. De Gaulle began to attend Good Samaritan Free Church regularly. In 2005 the couple reconciled, and Mrs. De Gaulle attended services regularly with Mr. De Gaulle. Counseling from the church contributed to assisting the couple to develop marital boundaries that prevented relatives from interfering in marital matters. Since 2005 the couple has attended a home group, Sunday school services, and Sunday worship services and participated fully in the church community. The couple believes that joining the church grounded them and matured them as a couple. Following the psychotherapy of 2004 and 2005, they credit their church community with helping them adjust to an adult level of mutual respect, communication, and appropriate marital adjustment. Both were baptized on the same day in 2006. They attend at least 2 church functions a week. Importantly, Mr. De Gaulle enjoys the ongoing mentoring and counsel of Pastor Anthony M—in whom he still confides regarding transient marital adjustment issues and any other psychosocial stressors.

Nothing on the church's website, reviewed 4/23/15, indicates that the community has health-negative characteristics, such as cultic leanings, fanaticism, extremism, despised enemies, etc. The church appears to provide a panoply of pro-social, health-positive programs that involve worship, small groups, service projects, spiritual teaching, and ethical role modeling.

Family, Childhood, and Developmental History

Mr. De Gaulle's family of origin is intact. His father is Burton De Gaulle, born 1946. His mother is Cathy De Gaulle, born 1949. He has a younger brother, Fritz, with whom he enjoyed a close relationship in boyhood. He recalls being picked on in elementary school and experiencing some bullying. He met his future wife, however, in the seventh grade and graduated from high school with above-average grades in math and science classes. In adulthood, he maintains friendships that began in high school.

Sexual abuse complicated Mr. De Gaulle's early life. Mr. De Gaulle reported that he was raped as a child by a neighbor six to eight years older than himself. Mr. De Gaulle reports that the abuse may have lasted from age 5 until 11. He then put a stop to the abuse by avoiding the abuser. He also reports that he suffered the experience of a male relative making him feel uncomfortable by inappropriately touching him. Although he has no recollection of the male relative sexually assaulting him, Mr. De Gaulle reports that he was simply made uncomfortable by the male relative's attention to his body and touching his legs. He further remarked that he went through a period of wishing his father had been more protective of him in general. Like many young men who have suffered sexual abuse, Mr. De Gaulle coped with the pain of the childhood abuse by repressing it.

Following his concussion in 1997, Mr. De Gaulle experienced a return of the repressed material of the sexual abuse of his boyhood. He experienced shame and nightmares informed by abuse-related material. He worried that the experience may have undermined his ability to enjoy normal marital intimacy, and he experienced shame.

Fortunately, the hospitalization of 1999 began a healing journey. Mr. De Gaulle was able to disclose his concerns about the abuse to Dr. Mary Q. Subsequently, he discussed aspects of the pain of the experience with all three of the psychotherapists listed above. He further was able to work though elements of the abuse material with his spiritual advisors from Good Samaritan Free Church. Importantly for this evaluation is the fact that Mr. De Gaulle notes that his religious convictions preclude him from acting out against a real or imagined abuser in the form of vigilante justice.

When recent sexual scandal rocked the graduate school (a well-respected academic had been exposed as acting out pedophilically for years), Mr. De Gaulle reflected again on his own abuse experiences and discussed these issues with the support of his church community and family of origin. He also initiated conversations with his father that helped them both to understand and resolve at the adult level that as a boy Mr. De Gaulle would have liked more protection from his father. Mr. De Gaulle handled feelings aroused by the scandal deliberately, rather than impulsively.

From hard therapeutic effort, clinical working through, spiritual counsel, and appropriate communication, Mr. De Gaulle has made an ally of Mrs. De Gaulle in this area. The couple reports that they enjoy all the benefits of normal married life.

Schooling

As noted Mr. De Gaulle attended Kindergarten through twelfth grade in County School District.

From 1988 to 1993, the client studied Mechanical Engineering at Charter University and successfully completed his BS Degree.

From 2007 until the present, he has been a Masters of Sciences Candidate in Environmental Science, also at Charter University. His current grade point average is 3.74. His MS Thesis is titled [ ]. After completing his MS, he will pursue a PhD in the same field.

Mr. De Gaulle's research interests involve disease issues of native fish and the impact of introduction of foreign fish to the native water systems and the impacts of navigation facilities on darters in major rivers.

His publications are relevant to his field of study. In 2010, he was listed as second author following his academic advisor in a technical report commissioned and published by the military.

Since 2009, he has made four major academic/professional presentations to internationally recognized professional groups.

Occupational

Mr. De Gaulle worked in a fast-food restaurant from 1987 to 1992. From 1992 to 1994, he worked in a home remodeling retail store and supported operations by developing inventory and invoicing computer systems. In 1995, he purchased a portable sawmill and ran a business that specialized in woodwork at job sites. From 1999 to 2004, he specialized in tile and commercial flooring. He reports that a downturn in the industry which, combined with physical strain from injuries, led him to return to school to pursue graduate work. With his wife's corroboration, he noted that he had a good reputation as a contractor and was never fired from a job.

From 2008 until the present, Mr. De Gaulle has been employed as a Graduate Research Assistant in the Environmental Science Lab at Charter University. His duties include teaching science core requirements to undergraduates and conducting original research.

Available academic and occupational data indicates that Mr. De Gaulle is temperamentally diligent and achieves at a high level.

Medical

In 1986, at age 16, Mr. De Gaulle underwent successful corrective surgery for a "lazy eye." In 1991, he suffered a bike wreck on Charter's campus. At County Community Hospital, he was treated for lacerations and concussion. For a few months, he experienced headaches and blurry vision.

In 1997, Mr. De Gaulle broke his shoulder in a sawmill accident. That same year, a forklift accident left him with a concussion. Mr. De Gaulle was then treated by both a neurologist, Dr. O, and his primary physician. Medical issues stemming from the forklift accident included night sweats, nightmares, insomnia, neck and back pain, and vulnerability to stress with signs and symptoms of depression, anxiety, and anger present. Mr. De Gaulle believes that the antidepressant medication he took at the time may have been prescribed to treat some of his sleep issues. The closed head injury that Mr. De Gaulle experienced appears to have injured his mental and physical health, but not permanently.

In 1999, he was treated by Dr. Arthur L for gastroenteritis. An Associate Professor of Family and Community Medicine at the Gloria

Lazar Medical Center, College of Medicine, Dr. Arthur L remains Mr. De Gaulle's primary physician.

In a letter dated 4/4/13, Dr. L writes:

[Mr. De Gaulle] had a temporary marital disruption following this closed head injury episode … His marital problems have long since resolved and he has been living haply [sic] with his wife for the last 12 or so years. These symptoms and signs of depression, anxiety, and anger issues have since cleared, and have not recurred in the more than dozen years since. There has not been any reason these years to have any concerns about Mr. De Gaulle's ability to use a firearm safely and appropriately…In the time I have known him since, I have not found any reason to question his safety to himself or others in owning or using a firearm.

During a 4/7/15 phone consultation with this evaluator, Dr. L corroborated that he had written the letter that is excerpted above. He also affirmed that he finds no clinical evidence that Mr. De Gaulle exhibits a mental or physical problem that would prohibit him from using firearms safely. He offered that Mr. De Gaulle is an apparently healthy man who takes no prescription medications.

Other Relevant History

Drug and Alcohol

The record is negative for significant drug or alcohol history. Mr. De Gaulle drinks socially but in negligible amounts.

Criminal

He was served with a PFA in 1999 and 2004 following flare-ups in marital contention. Somewhat embarrassed, Mrs. De Gaulle reported that she regrets initiating both PFAs and that she never believed that Mr. De Gaulle actually threatened or endangered her. In retrospect, she believes that she was pressured by a problematic, meddlesome relative to initiate these actions. Subsequently, with therapeutic effort and support from her church community, she has individuated from this relative and has drawn quite close to Mr. De Gaulle. Other than being served these dubiously motivated PFAs, Mr. De Gaulle reports no significant criminal record or history, and I have found none in the record. He reports a history negative for fighting and has never been in a lawsuit. He denies ever being investigated for a crime.

Firearms

The Intake dated 3/26/13 asked Mr. De Gaulle to briefly explain his lifelong experience with firearms, including mentoring, weapons training, hunting, military, and other such experiences. He wrote:

> I was taught from a very young age by my father to safely handle and respect firearms. I am a hunter and outdoorsman. I passed the hunters safety course at 12 years old. I was a Boy Scout attaining rank of Life, one step below Eagle. I have continued to hunt off and on throughout my adult life and to shoot recreationally with friends and family. I was teaching my wife proper gun handling and safely as my father taught me until I discovered the 302 on my record. Since then I have taken an about-face so as not to further hinder my chances of remedying this in a timely fashion by legal means.

Mr. De Gaulle presents as a man without significant drug, alcohol, or criminal history—who, although experienced with weapons—is candid about his good-faith effort to abide by the letter of the law regarding his handling of firearms. Third-party informants corroborate a history absent of delinquency and some note that they have observed Mr. De Gaulle operate firearms appropriately at a shooting range.

Mental Status and Behavioral Observations

Mr. De Gaulle arrived with Mrs. De Gaulle to the examination 15 minutes early. Dressed casually like a graduate student, he was candid and forthcoming throughout the interview. Affectively expressive, Mr. De Gaulle demonstrated appropriate emotional responses throughout the interview; he looked transiently distressed, for example, discussing episodes of marital discord; he looked serious and respectful describing his relationship to the Reverend Dr. Anthony M; he looked pained, but determined to disclose, when queried about childhood abuse; he was intense and emphatic—but not exaggerated—when describing his Christian religious and ethical commitments. His flow of speech was that of a normal person. There was no evidence of depression, disproportionate anxiety, dissociation, delusions, hallucinations, or attention problems. Throughout the interview he presented as a reliable historian and looked thoughtful or concerned if an exact time for a remote incident did not immediately come to mind. By history and graduate school performance he has excellent intellectual resources. At times, he talked about the kind of career he would enjoy and appeared hopeful. No indicators of anger or hostility or suspiciousness were present. When asked, Mr. De Gaulle explicitly denied recent or remote homicidal or suicidal intent or ideation.

As a couple, the De Gaulles presented as a well-adjusted, cooperative spousal unit operating as a team. Both took turns and helped each other with reporting. Both were interviewed briefly alone and convincingly denied being unduly influenced or coerced by the absent spouse. The couple denied that Mr. De Gaulle suffered behavioral dyscontrol (the inability to control one's behavior) that might be born of a traumatic brain injury, and there was no evidence of such a problem during the interview. The couple remained consistent reporting their belief that Mr. De Gaulle has never been a genuinely dangerous person.

Third-Party Information

For a psychological examination of this sort, obtaining third-party information represents a necessary component of responsible data gathering. One authoritative tome remarks, "… third-party information is a mandatory component of most forensic evaluations."[9] To this end, at the start of these processes, this examiner asked Mr. De Gaulle to obtain letters from people who have known him for a number of years in a number of venues. Parties directly familiar with Mr. De Gaulle's

---

[9] Gary B. Melton, John Petrila, Norman G. Poythress, and Christopher Slobogin, *Psychological Evaluations for the Courts: A Handbook for Mental Health Professionals and Lawyers*. 3rd edition (New York: Guilford Press, 2007), 53.

performance in family life, university work, church life, and so forth were asked to opine regarding their impression of his soundness of mind and ability to safely manage firearms. It was further established that the letter writers should expect that this evaluator would contact them via phone to corroborate that they, in fact, wrote the letters and that additional questions about Mr. De Gaulle might be asked.

Seven letters were generated by eight parties; informants included Mr. De Gaulle's parents (who co-signed a letter), in addition to his wife, friend, neighbor, pastor, academic advisor, and physician. All parties affirmed that as they know Mr. De Gaulle they experience him to be mentally sound and they believe that he will be safe with firearms. While the informants may be presumed to be biased toward Mr. De Gaulle's wishes, it might also be assumed that if any of them had reservations regarding his mental stability and capacity to manage arms, they might have voiced them—either out of concern for his own well-being or community safety. All letters were corroborated via phone.

Psychological Tests Administered and Results

Minnesota Multiphasic Personality Inventory-2 (MMPI-2)

Mr. De Gaulle was administered the MMPI-2. He was mailed the test, filled out the 567-item measure of psychopathology in forced-choice or true-false format, and returned the test via mail. My practice then faxed the score card to the professionally accepted scorer of this test, Pearson Assessments. Pearson Assessments scored the test and faxed this examiner the scores and a computer-generated narrative. During the clinical interview, Mr. De Gaulle affirmed that he could swear under oath that it was he who had taken the MMPI-2.

Arguably the most researched test of psychopathology in the world, Pope, et al. (2006) provides reasons for using the test in court: it offers personality information on defendants or litigants whose mental health must be determined; the true false questions are easy to understand; computerized scoring ensures the test's objectivity; it is normed for Americans; it measures test taking style—such as faking good or bad and defensiveness—and offers validity scales; it offers a variety of clinical scales for pathology, a high score on which is associated with specific behavioral characteristics; the test is reliable and valid; the test helps practitioners to predict behavior.[10] Melamed, et al. (2011) recommend the MMPI-2 to assess the risk of violent behavior prior to the issuance of a permit to carry a handgun.[11]

While the full report is appended, important excerpts from Mr. De Gaulle's computer generated MMPI-2 computer generated report are as follows:

Profile Validity: This clinical profile has marginal validity because the client attempted to place himself in an overly positive light by minimizing faults and denying psychological problems ... His defensiveness on the MMPI-2 may be better understood by examining the S [Superlative Self-Presentation] subscale elevations. He approached the test items with a view toward presenting himself as being very serene in his approach to life. His high score on the Serenity subscale suggests that he would like to be viewed as having no problems or pressure. Moreover, he obtained a high elevation on S3 (Contentment with Life), suggesting that he wants to appear to others as happy and contented with his present situation.

Symptomatic Patterns: His MMPI-2 clinical and content scales are within normal limits. No clinical symptoms were reported.

Interpersonal Relations: Quite outgoing and sociable, he has a strong need to be around others ... He views his home life in a generally positive manner; he reports that it is pleasant and problem-free. He tends to feel strong emotional support from those close to him.

Diagnostic Considerations: This client's clinical profile is within normal limits and no diagnostic considerations are provided.

---

[10] Kenneth S. Pope, James N. Butcher, and Joyce Seelen, *The MMPI, MMPI-2, and MMPI-A in Court: A Practical Guide for Expert Witnesses and Attorneys,* 3rd edition (Washington, DC: American Psychological Association, 2006).

[11] Y. Melamed, A. Bauer, M. Kalian, P. Rosca, and R. Mester, "Assessing the Risk of Violent Behavior Before Issuing a License to Carry a Handgun," *Journal of the American Academy of Psychiatry and Law* (39, 4) 2011, 543-548.

Like many high-performing professionals whose work and values demand high performance in multiple arenas, Mr. De Gaulle took the test in the so-called defensive manner. Mr. De Gaulle's experience of multiple selection processes and durably high performance in his exacting university work makes him analogous to well-adjusted groups of professionals who—while underreporting distress on this instrument—are still considered well-adjusted. For example, Pope, et al. remark, "In general, typical airline pilots tend to be well-adjusted. They usually have been prescreened or preselected, and most come through rigorous military screening programs … most are extremely defensive and take the MMPI with a response set to present a non-pathological pattern."[12]

The pilots' "defensive" response pattern—especially as indicated by K and S validity scales—would be associated with the diligent, well-adjusted professionals' characteristic of putting their best foot forward—even on a psychological test. Mr. De Gaulle's professional situation and test-taking style are similar to this group.

Another interpretive consideration of Mr. De Gaulle's MMPI-2 score involves his religious involvement and his low clinical-scale scores. Clinical scales measure Hypochondriasis, Depression, Conversion-Hysteria, Psychopathic Deviance, and other mental problems. High clinical scores are associated with higher probabilities of psychopathology. But research suggests a negative association between test-taker religious involvement and clinical-scale scores. Conducting exploratory research with a sample of undergraduate college students, MacDonald and Holland (2003) observe, "… persons reporting involvement in organized religion obtained significantly lower MMPI-2 clinical scale scores and were found to be less likely to obtain a clinically significant score."[13] They further note, "… religion is associated with increased healthy behaviors, social support and an enhanced sense of meaning and coherence, three factors known to have a direct impact on levels of psychopathology and psychological distress."[14] Since 2004, Mr. De Gaulle has been involved in organized religion

---

[12] Pope et al, *MMPI*, 17.

[13] Douglas A. MacDonald and Daniel Holland, "Spirituality and the MMPI-2," *Journal of Clinical Psychology*, 59, (March 17, 2003), 399.

[14] MacDonald and Holland, "Spirituality," 408.

habitually; it may be that he experiences the health-positive benefits of organized religion and that his low clinical-scale scores reflect good adjustment—in part attributable to that consistent religious involvement.

To sum, Mr. De Gaulle took the testing with a defensive style not dissimilar to well-adjusted, diligent, professionals. Religiously involved, his clinical scale scores fell below the level significant for psychopathology. Mr. De Gaulle's MMPI-2 was negative for psychopathology and offered no diagnostic considerations. Overall, Mr. De Gaulle's MMPI-2 profile offers a metrical depiction of a psychologically healthy man who wishes to present himself in a positive light.

Beck Depression Inventory-II (BDI-II)

On this professionally accepted screen for depression for the past 2 weeks prior to the examination, Mr. De Gaulle's BDI-II was insignificant for depression.

Beck Anxiety Inventory (BAI)

On this professionally accepted screen for anxiety for the past 1 week prior to the examination, Mr. De Gaulle's BAI was insignificant for anxiety.

Summary

Mr. De Gaulle seeks to obtain the Commonwealth's approval to remove his firearms disability. During a marital dispute in 1999 following a 2-year period of ill health, Mr. De Gaulle made an ill-chosen but unserious remark about self-destruction born of exasperation and was involuntarily hospitalized. From 1999 to 2006, he responsibly attended to his mental and physical health. He retained two psychotherapists and a marital counselor. He worked with a neurologist and collaborated with his primary care physician. He also consulted professionals regarding his childhood sexual abuse and subsequently took his wife, pastor, and father into his confidence. His history is positive for appropriately addressing that quite personal matter. He and his wife resolved their differences and joined a lively Free Church community that is likely to provide ongoing health benefits to Mr. De Gaulle, who is quite active in his church. Following an early history of bullying, Mr. De Gaulle made a successful social adjustment and appears to enjoy a number of long-term friendships.

A graduate student in Environmental Science, Mr. De Gaulle has a number of publications and responsibilities which demonstrate a conscientious, diligent work style and temperament. His medical record culminates with his primary care physical finding Mr. De Gaulle healthy in mind and body and capable of safely handling firearms. Mr. De Gaulle has no significant drug or alcohol history. In the past, he has received firearm safety training and has a history positive for safely handling firearms. During the clinical interview, he and his wife presented in a manner consistent with a well-adjusted couple. Both affirmed their belief that Mr. De Gaulle has never been a dangerous person. Mr. De Gaulle's observable mental status was that of an intelligent man with a bright affect who disclosed and behaved appropriately. No signs of relevant clinical syndromes or character pathology or gross neurological signs were evidenced. He took the MMPI-2 with a defensive style that sometimes characterizes diligent professionals, and he had no elevated scores indicative of psychopathology. The computerized report found his profile to be within normal limits and considered that Mr. De Gaulle has no diagnosis. Screens for depression and anxiety symptoms were also negative. While Mr. De Gaulle's history is positive for not uncommon psychological and adjustment problems, he has reasonably resolved them. He appears happily married, professionally accomplished, physically healthy, and mentally sound.

Answering the Referral Questions

a) If the applicant, Mr. De Gaulle, were to possess firearms, he will possess the firearms without risk to the applicant's self or any other person.
b) Mr. De Gaulle evidences no mental disorder and therefore has no diagnosis; he is mentally healthy and likely to remain so.

Conclusion

Thank you for the opportunity to examine Mr. De Gaulle and to provide these findings.

Charles L. Zeiders, Psy.D.
Clinical & Forensic Psychologist

****

Reflections on This Case
Interview with Dr. Douglas Schoeninger

Dr. Douglas Schoeninger: The popular mind sometimes sees expert witnesses as "hired guns." What prevents you professionally and spiritually from allowing your clinical opinion to be bought?

Dr. Charles Zeiders: Professionally, expert witnesses are obligated to answer the legal referral question in keeping with generally accepted methodologies, science, and theory. Our obligation is to the truth of the matter. To allow one's opinion to be bought by money or liking or disliking something related to the case is to lose objectivity. Such a thing would be a calamity for clinical integrity. Our ethical mission must always be clinical truth, as best as we can approximate that truth with our data and methodology. To *charge* for the time it takes to derive an opinion is reasonable and customary. But to *sell* an opinion is a grave legal and ethical transgression. The best forensic psychologists and psychiatrists always keep themselves on a short ethical leash.

From a Christian viewpoint, the "hired gun" infraction is even more calamitous. When God revealed the Ten Commandments to Moses, he was very clear about the matter of truth telling: "You shall not bear false witness against thy neighbor."[15] The theologian Richard McBrien observes that the "original aim of this commandment was to ensure truthful witness in law courts."[16] To distort clinical truth, or even the truth of one's expert opinion, under oath is not simply secular perjury, but a sin. McBrien's excellent commentary on the Ten Commandments finds that the edicts are "unconditional imperatives"[17] and an "enduring expression of natural law."[18] For an expert of faith, bearing false witness as a "hired gun" is simply not an option.

---

[15] Ex. 23:1

[16] McBrien, *Encyclopedia*, 333.

[17] McBrien, *Encyclopedia*, 331.

[18] McBrien, *Encyclopedia*, 334.

Schoeninger: What from the New Testament might also guide you spiritually as an expert?

Zeiders: Jesus observed that the truth will set us free.[19] In scriptural context, Jesus *is* the Truth that sets us free from the bondage of sin. On a high spiritual plane, accepting the salvific (leading to salvation) reality of Our Lord clears not only our consciences but also our fear of eternal judgment. We become free from metaphysical dread because of Christ and what he has accomplished for us on a cosmic level. For me, this sets the tone for my professional behavior. By doing my best as an expert, working in good faith to establish the best version of the clinical truth and then offering that to the legal process, I am free to offer my forensic best without the undue dread that an expert of bad faith might experience. Doing my job faithful to the facts frees me from being caught out. I don't want to overstate, though, that religious faith and clinical integrity fully remove some degree of anxiety from participating in the legal process. To give a forensic opinion is a matter of grave legal and social consequence.

Schoeninger: When you reflect on the anxiety you feel despite your attempts at faith in Christ and professional integrity, what does the Christian world offer to console you?

Zeiders: *The Catechism of the Catholic Church* offers a deeply consoling, germane message about the nature of difficult work. This message is beautiful, dignified, and reality-based. By enduring the hardship of work in union with Jesus, the carpenter of Nazareth and the one crucified on Calvary, man collaborates in a certain fashion with the Son of God in his redemptive work. He shows himself to be a disciple of Christ by carrying the cross daily in the work he is called to accomplish. Work can be a means of sanctification and way of animating earthly realties with the Spirit of Christ.[20]

---

[19] Jn 8:32

[20] *Catechism*, 643.

Schoeninger: How does spiritual discernment enter into your process of deciding to take a particular case and your sorting of the data as you are evaluating a case?

Zeiders: Spiritual discernment and professional ethics combine elegantly. If the retaining party convinces me that I will be allowed to provide a true clinical opinion without pressure to spin the facts in a partisan manner, I'm generally inclined to take the case. But I'm most moved to accept when I sense that my participation will accomplish an actual good, something that impacts the world to make it better. In Adlerian terms, "social interest" is my consideration. In Christian terms, a blessing of some sort must appear likely to emerge from my participation. Professionally, the probability of maintaining ethical faith with the facts, combined with inherent social good, represents my dual guiding criteria. But in terms of spiritual discernment, I'm drawn to cases wherein I can tell the truth and provide blessing. Even in gravely serious legal matters, telling the truth and providing blessings is a way—while remaining professionally appropriate—to be of some service to God and man, and hopefully to imitate Christ.

Schoeninger: Is your position similar to the Jungian notion of the hero's journey?

Zeiders: As attractive as it is, the Jungian idea of the hero-expert may give rise to ego inflation and grandiosity.[21] From the vantage of Christian depth psychology, the expert's role is organized best not in the hero's archetype but in the servant's role.

Schoeninger: Finally, your finding was that Mr. De Gaulle's mental health— perhaps his global health—transformed following his experience of God mediated through his religious community. Did De Gaulle bring any particular attitude to his new religion that was a game changer?

---

[21] Juan Antonio LaLlave and Thomas Gordon Gutheil, "Expert Witness and Jungian Arche- types," in *International Journal of Law and Psychiatry* (35), Oct. 2012, 456-463. www.research- gate.net/publication/232245626_Expert_witness_and_Jungian_archetypes.

Zeiders: I think so. He struck me as a bright man who was actually quite humble. Jung had something to say about humility and therapeutically hearing the voice of God.

> Christians often ask why God does not speak to them, as he is believed to have done in former days. When I hear such questions, it always makes me think of the rabbi who was asked how it could be that God often showed himself to people in the olden days while nowadays nobody ever sees him. The rabbi replied: "Nowadays there is no longer anybody who can bow low enough."[22]

Quite simply, Mr. De Gaulle bowed low enough. And that has made the difference.

---

[22] Carl G. Jung (ed.), *Man and His Symbols* (New York: Doubleday, 1964), 102.

CHAPTER TWO

A Plight Like Job's: Trauma, Grief, and Betrayal

Extreme suffering can bring us to question the very nature of existence. For a spiritual or religious person, this kind of suffering can bring despair and a loss of faith. At the same time, for someone emerging from grief and trauma, faith can be a resource. This chapter explores the nature of one patient's catastrophic experiences. It hypothesizes how depth psychology, engaged with his intact Catholic faith, might assist him to recover from the rape of his wife and the violent death of his son.

Introduction

Forensic psychology, which represents the intersection of mental health science and the justice system, often investigates extreme cases of calamity and suffering. Nodding to the frailty of human security, forensic psychology examines events from which the ordinary mind can shatter. The phone rings, and the world as we've known it vanishes. A lifetime of savings disappears, and one's financial advisor is unreachable. An aneurism destroys the industrious brain dreaming of a career in neuroscience. Reading emails of infidelity, the cuckold cocks his pistol. On sushi night, the FBI bursts into the executive suites, and the laughter stops. A paranoid leader subverts a liberal democracy and inaugurates epochal miseries. It's axiomatic that in our lives, something will go wrong, and suffering will be the result. Individual and collective disasters break upon us constantly and often shake the foundations of our metaphysical confidence.

For spiritual or religious people, misfortune can obliterate the capacity to sustain faith. Following the Holocaust, for example, some Jewish intellectuals declared that the Abrahamic covenant was no longer in force. The enormity of evil perpetrated by the Nazis against European Jewry exploded the notion that God kept faith with Israel. Emmanuel Levinas believed that the age of theologically credible explanations for suffering had come to an end with Auschwitz. Lionel Corbett observed:

> The Holocaust virtually confirmed Nietzsche's comment that God (at least the traditional image of God) is dead. For Levinas, the Holocaust cannot be assimilated into any meaningful conceptual system. … Other Holocaust writers also believe that the Holocaust is so conceptually unmanageable that our traditional ways of thinking no longer apply. As Cohen puts it, the Holocaust "has no meaning, because it denies meaning and makes a mockery of meaning."[23]

It's natural to seek health, prosperity, and security, but when the unthinkable happens, an individual or even a culture is at risk for despair. The evil of a disaster may fragment a person psychologically and leave him or her adrift in the cosmos. People might feel abandoned by God and exhibit signs and symptoms of illness. Anyone who has ever suffered (which, of course, means all of us) will feel more than a modicum of sympathy for the wretched fate of the biblical Job, whose misery is said to have derived from God allowing the devil to destroy the poor man's life as part of a bet. The devil killed Job's children and ruined his livelihood. His advisors told him it was his fault, and his raging wife told him to curse God and die. It's no wonder that this unfortunate soul developed physical and mental symptoms. Theologian Victor White observes, "[Job's] sufferings are truly frightful, but they are also symptoms; and the loss of his domesticated animals and his children … and his psychosomatic eruptions … add up to a clear clinical picture. He cannot cope. He retires

---

[23] Lionel Corbett and James Hollis, *The Anguish of the Soul: Psychotherapeutic Approaches to Suffering* (Asheville, NC: Chiron Publications, 2015), 197.

to the dunghill, the libido [life energy] is introverted, and he is in the grips of intense … depression."[24]

The problem of suffering like Job's, and finding psychological and spiritual solutions, has perennially preoccupied theologians and depth psychologists—especially depth psychologists who treat religious patients—because life's temporal disasters challenge the experience of meaning. What might help the afflicted find a way forward? If faith is shaken, can faith play a role in post-traumatic recovery?

These questions were on my mind as I finished the report below. The subject, one Hans Manheim (his name, like all names and identifying information in this blinded report, is pseudonymous), was a man who suffered as Job did. A practicing Catholic with a large family, Mr. Manheim had functioned well enough in his work and family life. He navigated family emergencies and worked diligently as a deli manager to fulfill his roles as husband, father, and breadwinner. Then the unthinkable happened. His wife, Paula, suffered a series of sexual assaults from her spiritual advisor. To escape accountability, the rapist fled the country while his religious order's attorneys obstructed inquires. Her assault tore open old wounds in both Hans and Paula Manheim.

On the heels of this tragedy, another struck. Of their children, Michael was the brightest star. Fascinated by animals, he'd accepted a position as an animal trainer at a poorly run traveling road show. Unbeknown to Michael or his parents, the manager of the show was notorious for violating animal safety regulations. During a performance (for which Michael was forbidden to prepare), two poorly cared-for grizzly bears tore him to pieces. In the face of these catastrophes, Mr. Manheim decompensated. (When a system is "compensated," it's able to function despite stressors and shortcomings. *Decompensation* describes an inability to compensate for these.)

As a husband and father, he simply collapsed, and his work as a deli manager suffered. Litigation around his work ability (or disability) ensued, and his attorney, Mr. Scooter Placidus, through his psychologist, Dr. Emma Swanson, reached out to me for forensic and psycho-diagnostic

---

[24] Quoted in Ann Conrad Lammers and Adrian Cunningham (eds.), *The Jung-White Letters*. New York: Routledge, 2007), 349.

testing. They sought a report that would answer the question whether the distressed man was capable of working, a determination relevant to an upcoming court case. In addition, Dr. Swanson, concerned about her patient's inability to regain intellectual, emotional, and behavioral equilibrium, sought a diagnostic second opinion and treatment recommendations geared toward stabilizing him.

At the time I was drafting the following forensic report, Mr. Manheim was in crisis. I dutifully answered the referral questions about his diagnoses, stabilization, and work capacity. I did not address what was not asked, which was to opine about Mr. Manheim's soul or whether a depth psychology that honored his bruised yet intact Catholic faith might help him. If, as St. John says, faith is the victory that overcomes the world,[25] how might psychotherapy *based on Manheim's faith* help him overcome these massive blows? I *will* venture an opinion on this in the interview with Douglas Schoeninger of the *Journal of Christian Healing* that follows this report.

Forensic Psychological Report [blinded]

Client: Hans Manheim
Date of evaluation: 1/4/16
Evaluator: Charles Zeiders, Psy.D., Clinical & Forensic Psychologist
Date of report: 1/8-10/16
Persons present: Hans Manheim, Paula, and Evaluator

Sources of information:
A. *Documents and Records*
Review of Intake Information completed by Hans Manheim on 12/13/16
Review of Treatment Summary and Progress Notes compiled by the subject's psychotherapist, Dr. Emma Swanson, dated 12/17/16
B. *Clinical Instruments*
Minnesota Multiphasic Personality Inventory-2 (MMPI-2)
Beck Depression Inventory II (BDI-II)
Beck Anxiety Inventory (BAI)

---

[25] 1 Jn 5: 4-5

Depression Checklist (from Intake Information form)
PTSD Symptom Scale – Interview (PSS-I)
Saint Louis University Mental Status Examination (SLUMS)
C. *Other*
Phone consultation with psychotherapist Dr. Swanson 12/23/16
Clinical interview with Hans and Paula Manheim 1/4/17

Reason for Referral and Purpose of Evaluation

Hans Manheim was referred to this practice by his psychotherapist Dr. Emma Swanson. Since 5/7/15, Mr. Manheim has attended 15 psychotherapeutic treatment sessions with Dr. Swanson that have lasted from 1 to 3 hours. During those sessions Mr. Manheim presented as diagnostically complex with symptomatology consistent with Post-Traumatic Stress Disorder (PTSD), depression, anxiety, impulsivity, insomnia, anger, and other symptoms. Records indicate a patient manifesting intense clinical distress with impairment in familial and occupational functioning. Additionally, his psychosocial stressors are multiple, including family discord, severe problems with work, financial problems, and embroilment in 3 lawsuits—one involves suit against a Roman Catholic institution and relates to a sexual assault perpetrated upon his wife Paula. The second involves a wrongful death suit against a business culpable for harboring dangerous animals that directly caused a grown son's horrifying death. The third (for which this report is immediately relevant) involves an action against an entity who may be liable to pay monies related to Mr. Manheim's employment problems.

Dr. Swanson (in conjunction with Scooter Placidus, Esq.) asked that this practice provide psychological testing, clinical interviewing, and evaluation to provide:

a) diagnostic and treatment advice relevant to Mr. Manheim's immediate stabilization,

b) and to opine as to Mr. Manheim's ability to return to work.

Identification

Hans Manheim is a 50-year-old (DOB: 7/25/66) Caucasian male. He lives with his wife Paula at 52 Cherry Lynn Lane, Pittsburgh, PA 15201.

Their family includes George, 28, who has a mate and a child and serves in the Army; Michael, 24, who is deceased, killed by grizzly bears at an animal show at which he worked; Savannah, 23, who is married; and Joseph, 20, who serves in the Marines. Children still living at home include Amanda, 18; Grace, 16; Paige, 12; Martina, 6; and Isadora, 3.

On the Intake form, Mr. Manheim also noted that he and his wife suffered 1 abortion and 4 miscarried children. Mr. Manheim presents as suffering from unresolved grief around these losses.

Prior to going on disability, Mr. Manheim worked as a Deli Manger at a Foster's Food Market.

He describes himself as a staunch Roman Catholic.

Presenting Problems

At the time of this writing Mr. Manheim reports diverse, intense signs and symptoms. On the Intake form he listed them as "anger, rage, depression, unclear thinking, problem solving, lack of focus or concentration, lack of empathy … isolation, suicidal thoughts, murderous thoughts, inability to complete tasks, control issues (inability to delegate), superiority complex …."

Questioned about his lethal thoughts Mr. Manheim denied gross dangerousness to himself or others and denied suicidal or homicidal plans. By "superiority complex," he noted that he worries that he is selfish—a negative self-assessment not uncommon among depressed patients. Mr. Manheim further wrote:

> Although I have experienced all these to greater or lesser degree over my entire life—things really started to fall apart for me after my wife was raped in March 2015 … and then in November 2015, one of my sons was mauled to death by grizzly bears where he worked. In April 2016, I was asked to decide if I wanted to leave the company I worked for 6 years as a manager or be demoted to a full-time employee. My therapist removed me from work on disability.

Summary of Previous Medical Treatment

Mr. Manheim reports a relatively unremarkable medical treatment history. His primary care physician is one Dr. Albert Ford.

His last physical exam may have been in the summer of 2014. Findings indicated that Mr. Manheim enjoys physical health with the exception of a pre-hypertensive condition.

Importantly, Mr. Manheim prefers alternative remedies to established treatments. He writes, "I rarely use medicine—prefer natural/homeopathic remedies. ... I am currently on a supplement regimen to detoxify my body based on hair analysis."

Summary of Mental Health Treatment History

Until retaining Dr. Swanson, Mr. Manheim had no significant mental health treatment history. He has never retained a psychiatrist, and he has never undergone psychiatric hospitalization.

Under the strain of mounting psychosocial stressors and intense signs and symptoms, Mr. Manheim entered psychotherapeutic treatment. Dr. Swanson summarizes the treatment as follows:

> In March 2015, Hans Manheim's wife Paula entered an intensive live-in trauma treatment program. She did remarkably well in that program, and as she began to improve and regain her role and responsibilities as a mother, Hans's deep trauma surfaced in a more serious way. It is not uncommon for a caretaker with many responsibilities to reach a breaking point as the non-functioning spouse begins to improve in function. Since April 2015, Hans began to exhibit more serious symptoms of complex PTSD which was exacerbated by increasing paranoia as he experienced difficulties related to his performance, temper and agitation at his place of employment.
>
> Hans's family has endured many levels of trauma for an extended and prolonged period of time. Initial intervention has and will continue to consist of individual and marital counseling, collaborative problem solving, parenting and psycho-educational interventions to understand the dynamics of trauma and abuse, the development and maintenance of

respectful boundaries and open supportive communication together with consequence planning and Cognitive Behavioral Therapy (CBT).

Since his family has been impacted by the traumatic death of their son Michael who was mauled by two grizzly bears (the poor lad was an animal trainer at a traveling road show, at which he was ripped to pieces before an audience of horrified children). It's been a year of intense grief and mourning.

In addition, his wife Paula recently disclosed repeated sexual assaults by a priest, and Hans has been trying to manage the catastrophe of her ongoing sexual trauma, which has been particularly disturbing in light of his wife's dramatic history of childhood sexual abuse. Together they initiated subsequent legal proceedings and criminal investigations which are ongoing.

Since April 2015, Hans has entered an intensive psychotherapeutic process to accomplish the grief and healing work necessary to recover.

It has also been critical to teach him anger management and resolution/reconciliation skills to calm his overactive limbic system from the impulse to react with trauma-driven impulses to fight, freeze, flee or fawn during incidents where he is overwhelmed by a pervasive sense of powerlessness. These stresses are compounded by debts, medical expenses and monthly rent with the fears of unemployment and a large family to care for.

From her work with Mr. Manheim, Dr. Swanson has developed the following diagnostic hypotheses:

Post-Traumatic Stress Disorder
Adjustment Disorder with Mixed Anxiety and Depressed Mood
Relational Problem Not Otherwise Specified
Partner Relational Problem
Relational Problem Related to a Mental Disorder or General Medical Condition
Parent-Child Relational Problem

On the medical model, of course, treatment follows diagnosis, and treatment interventions appear to sensibly address the diagnostic entities enumerated. For example, Mr. Manheim suffers insomnia—a symptom not uncommon among traumatized, depressed patients—and treatment provided a 16-week cognitive behavioral module to promote restorative sleep. Treatment also tailored cognitive behavioral interventions to address anxiety and mood symptoms and to provide Mr. Manheim with self-soothing and relational strategies to decrease impulsivity and hyper arousal and to improve his ability to relate calmly with his wife and children who have also been deleteriously impacted by family tragedies such as death and sexual abuse. Treatment appears to recognize that Mr. Manheim is embedded in a highly stressed and very tense family system. Interventions enable Mr. Manheim to function more adaptively within the system while also positively contributing to its wellness. Dr. Swanson's notes indicate that she and Mr. Manheim are adequately aware of safety considerations for all parties.

Family, Childhood, and Developmental History

Born in Rochester, Maine, Mr. Manheim was born into an intact family. He lived with his parents, 2 sisters, and 4 brothers. He was the 2nd-to-youngest child. He reports little recollection of his early years. He believes however, that a 1st-degree relative sexually molested him and a brother prior to the age of ten.

Schooling

Attending local parochial and public schools, Mr. Manheim earned his high school diploma and attended 2 years of college.

Occupational

Having married Paula, with a growing family for which to provide, Mr. Manheim discontinued his education and went to work. Among his early jobs was a position as a beer salesman at which he was successful.

Following a family crisis, Mr. Manheim moved his family from Maine to Pennsylvania, where he worked for five years as manager in a food store. He then he left that position and assumed a similar position for Foster's. The crises of Paula's sexual assault and Michael's death correlate with the dissatisfaction that Mr. Manheim's superiors appear to have expressed with his performance.

Importantly, Mr. Manheim reports a job history characterized by generally positive performance reviews. He and Paula agreed that he spent a great deal of time at work and appeared to draw a great deal of satisfaction from it. Both agree that he overworked and under functioned as a husband and father.

Other Important Information

Possibly due to embarrassment—or defensiveness—the couple had difficulty discussing what appeared to be a history of clinically significant sexual issues. What I was able to learn was that both husband and wife believe that as children, their sexualities were interfered with by bad actors. As mentioned, Hans believes that a first-degree relative molested him during boyhood.

Also, early in the last decade, Hans and Paula report that they learned that their children had been directly or indirectly impacted by sexual abusers. They reported the matter to authorities who were ultimately unable to help either the couple or their children gain justice or treatment. The couple reported that they believe authorities mishandled the investigation and frightened the entire family system with a threatening and insensitive investigatory manner. When authorities concluded the matter around 2004, Mr. Manheim moved the family to Pennsylvania. He has never spoken to a mental health professional about his personal experiences during that upsetting episode or about his concerns for his wife and family.

Both husband and wife noted on several occasions that their intimate life and marital friendship is undermined by Mr. Manheim's oversexed and possibly sexually compulsive behavior toward Paula. Importantly, the couple was only able to provide a vague, impressionistic history about this sexual issue and sexual traumas. Nothing led me to believe that the children living at home are in any danger. I was led to believe that Mr. Manheim has never processed these important matters in a way that made his relationship to them clear and uncomplicated. Further assessment in this area is required.

Also, that Mr. Manheim believes that he experienced some sort of sexual abuse during his formative years is clinically important. Many people who possess this belief suffer from profound and unresolved trauma that requires intensive and protracted psychotherapy. It is also important to note that many patients of this sort decompensate between the ages of 40 and 50 when various life experiences strip them of their defenses.

Spiritual and Religious History

Mr. Manheim believes that his staunch Roman Catholic faith will play a significant role in restoring his health. He noted that church teachings prevent him from committing suicide or homicide and challenge him to forgive the bad actors in his life. He notes that church teachings also challenge him to forgive himself for his perceived failings. Mr. Manheim and his family attend mass every week and engage in various church-sponsored social activities, like wine and cheese nights. He also noted that he had a spiritual director for the past 4 or 5 years—but that relationship has dwindled in recent months. When discussing his faith, Mr. Manheim's mostly anxious and depressed affect brightened considerably.

Other Relevant History

Drug and alcohol: Insignificant history by subject's report.
Criminal: Insignificant history by subject's report.

Psychological Tests Administered and Results

Minnesota Multiphasic Personality Inventory-2 (MMPI-2)

Mr. Manheim was administered the MMPI-2. He was mailed the test, filled out the 567-item measure of psychopathology in forced-choice or true-false format, and returned the test via mail. My practice then faxed the score card to the professionally accepted scorer of this test, Pearson Assessments. Pearson Assessments scored the test and faxed this examiner the raw scores and a computer-generated narrative. Pearson found that while Mr. Manheim demonstrated a slight tendency to answer False over True—regardless of content—and neglected to answer 5 items, his profile is probably valid and provides an adequate indication of his current personality functioning. (As a sample of behavior Mr. Manheim's tendency to select False may reflect the pronounced mental negativism characteristic of severely depressed and horrified patients.)

Elevations on MMPI-2 Scales:

On the MMPI-2 Clinical, Supplementary, and Content Scales the following scores were elevated—that is, in the "clinical" range.

Depression (D): This indicates low mood, unhappiness, and dysphoria (profound state of unease or dissatisfaction that may accompany depression, anxiety, or agitation); lack of drive and suicidal ideation are important clinical considerations here.

Psychopathic Deviate: This can indicate antisocial behavior, but in Mr. Manheim's case, it is more likely accounted for by tremendous family tension and alienation from self and society.

Paranoia: Elevations here can point to psychosis, but for this patient it more likely means that he feels like life gave him a raw deal, and he feels sensitive, suspicious, and guarded.

Psychothenia (a disorder characterized by phobias, obsessions, compulsions, or excessive anxiety): This elevation indicates symptomology where anxiety, tension, worry, and apprehension are present.

Schizophrenia: High scores can point to psychosis or unusual thoughts and attitudes as well as eccentricity and social alienation. Because Mr. Manheim's response style was insignificant for bizarre sensory experience or bizarre ideas, it is doubtful that he is formally psychotic. The elevation here is accounted for by answers that report alienation and lack of mastery over thoughts and impulses.

Social Introversion-Extroversion: The slight elevation here indicates that Mr. Manheim is more introverted than extroverted.

Post-Traumatic Stress Disorder Scale: Mr. Manheim's elevated score here is consistent with his existing diagnosis of PTSD.

Marital Distress Scale: The high score here is consistent with the experience of marital distress.

Anxiety: This elevated score suggests the presence of clinically significant anxiety.

Obsessiveness: This higher score suggests that Mr. Manheim may ruminate about his issues.

Depression (DEP): This scale is another MMPI-2 measure of depression. Mr. Manheim's score is elevated, and he may experience a significant number of negative, depressing thoughts and additional depressive symptoms.

Type A Scale: This slightly elevated score indicates the presence of some Type A characteristics that characterize hard-driving, fast-moving, work-oriented individuals. Mr. Manheim has competitive drive. He wants to succeed.

Low Self Esteem: The elevated score here indicates the presence of low self-esteem.

Family Problems Scale: The elevation here indicates that Mr. Manheim acknowledges significant family discord.

Work Interference Scale: The elevation here indicates the presence of some attitudes or behaviors that can drive poor work performance.

Negative Treatment Indicators Scale: This high score may indicate negative attitudes toward treatment. Low motivation, perhaps born of depression, as well as difficulty with disclosing should be explored.

Important Findings Excerpted from the Computerized MMPI-2 Interpretative Report
Profile Validity
"His MMPI-2 profile is probably valid ...."

Symptomatic Patterns

"... The client is likely to be moody, angry, distrustful, and quite resentful of others, possibly because he feels extremely insecure and inadequate and tends to blame others for his problems. Behavioral deterioration under stress is characteristic of individuals with this profile. ... He endorsed a number of items suggesting that he is experiencing low morale and a depressed mood. ... It is important to perform a suicide assessment ..."

Interpersonal Relations

"Poor social skills and disturbance in interpersonal relationships are hallmarks of such clients. He is overly sensitive and resistant to the demands of others, and he may be quite argumentative and obnoxious. He tries to stay aloof but may show dependency feelings and an exaggerated need for affection. He is very suspicious of others and rejects emotional ties. This client is probably behaving in unpredictable and erratic ways, which may produce a great deal of marital strain ..."

Diagnostic Considerations

"Many individuals with this profile receive a diagnosis of Schizophrenic Disorder. The possibility of an Affective Disorder or Personality Disorder should be considered, however ..."

Treatment Considerations

"Outpatients with this MMPI-2 profile are typically experiencing severe psychological problems and are frequently treated with psychotropic medication. ... Many such clients have extremely low self-esteem and do not seem to be able to alter their self-perceptions readily, even under conditions of positive feedback. Long-term treatment is probably necessary if significant gains are to be made ..."

"Psychological treatment of a focused, directive nature is likely to be more successful than insight-oriented treatment. Treatment may be aimed at symptom relief, stress reduction, and reality orientation by providing clear feedback about his typically poor social functioning in as supportive a therapeutic environment as possible ..."

Beck Depression Inventory-II (BDI-II)

On this professionally accepted screen for depression for the past 2 weeks, Mr. Manheim's score was 35. This indicates severe depression. When interviewed, he reported that he feels like a failure as a spouse and father, gets little pleasure from life, experiences guilt that his family is unhappy, feels punished, has disappointed himself, experiences indecisiveness about "everything," feels worthless, sleeps poorly, loses weight, and suffers fatigue.

Beck Anxiety Inventory (BAI)

On this professionally accepted screen for anxiety for the past 1 week, Mr. Manheim's score was 31; this indicates severe anxiety. When interviewed, he reported that his severe symptoms include an inability to relax, fear of the worst happening, terror, and nervousness. Other symptoms include feeling hot, a racing heart, shakiness, fears of losing control, and abdominal discomfort.

PTSD Symptom Scale—Interview (PSS-I)

On this measure of PTSD symptomatology for the past 2 weeks, Mr. Manheim had a clinically significant severity score of 22 and suffers from all the symptoms necessary to qualify for a formal diagnosis of PTSD. Because his symptoms have multiple traumatic etiologies (Paula's rape and Michael's terrible death), his PTSD should be considered complex. He suffers from intrusive thoughts from both traumas and noted an intense anniversary reaction a year after Paula's assault. This reaction involved both psychological and physical tension. He has lost interest in free-time activities since the trauma, exercised less, and abandoned recreational activities like playing games. He connects the traumas to a sense of pessimism about his career and marriage. Symptoms of post-traumatic hyperarousal are especially remarkable. He has difficulty falling asleep, suffers irritability and outbursts of anger (including a recent, frightening incident of road rage), has trouble concentrating, and demonstrates an exaggerated startle response. He also tends to be hypervigilant regarding the safety of his children, even when they are safely in the house.

Mental Status, Behavioral Observations, and Impressions

Mr. Manheim and his wife, Paula, entered my practice on time and casually dressed for our six-hour clinical interview on a snowy Saturday. His motor behavior was slightly slow. His flow of speech was appropriate but slowed at times to an absolute halt when discussing painful subjects, like his son's death. His attitude toward the process was cooperative. His mood was depressed and his affective expressions showed sadness and inner pain. His facial muscles were often quite tense, and then he would relax with a look of demoralization and quiet exhaustion. Corresponding to his expressions of pain and discomfort were topics of Paula's sexual assault and his son's untimely death. Discussing the latter, Mr. Manheim appeared to go into a brief, dissociative trance. It is a subject of almost unbearable pain for him.

Despite his MMPI-2 psychoticism score, Mr. Manheim demonstrated no gross delusions or hallucinations. But brief trancelike episodes to dull intense inner pain appeared present. Possibly because Mr. Manheim has untreated psychological issues that go back to earlier development and because these issues may be emotionally charged, Mr. Manheim's narrative stream did not flow normally. Much of the history he offered had only an impressionistic quality to it. By report, his behavior at home is one of dysphoric inactivity. A recent incident of road rage suggests some problems with impulse control. But his impulse control during the examination was normal.

Mr. Manheim demonstrated insight that much of his current distress is related to the horrifying shock of his wife's assault and son's death and the subsequent decline in his ability to work. He had further insight that his distress also involves the fact that there is discord within his family and that the relationship between he and his wife is exceptionally strained. Importantly, neither Mr. Manheim nor his wife could provide more than an imprecise, impressionistic history of sexual issues and traumas that Mr. Manheim and his wife and family may have experienced. Both made it clear, however, that their children are safe.

Mr. Manheim reported that he has few recollections of his childhood; therefore, repressed or dissociated issues from Mr. Manheim's early life cannot be ruled out. If there is a sleeping giant in Mr. Manheim's unconscious, it may erupt. He has little energy to defend against either internal or external stressors at the current moment. Because his depression, anxiety, and post-traumatic symptoms were so pronounced, I administered the *Saint Louis University Mental Status Examination* (SLUMS). I feared that his syndromes may have driven a pseudo-dementia, or a cognitive decline that mimics neurocognitive disorders. Despite his extreme psychological distress, Mr. Manheim obtained a perfect score on the SLUMS. He was oriented times three; short-term memory was intact; he could calculate, follow directions, and accurately manipulate information. His basic cognitive abilities were intact.

Summary

Mr. Manheim is a fifty-year-old white male, married to Paula, with grown children and children at home. He has little recollection for his early life but believes he was sexually abused by a first degree relative. He graduated from high school and attended two years of college. He married Paula and the couple had children. Over ten years ago, a sexual abuse incident followed by an upsetting investigation caused Mr. Manheim to move his family from Maine to Pennsylvania. The history given to this examiner was imprecise. But Mr. Manheim noted that he was upset by this incident.

He and his wife have a stressed relationship that involves sexual issues, but the couple was not able to fully delineate the exact nature of their marital problems or sexual issues. Mr. Manheim and his wife also reported that their family is distressed, but they had difficulty being specific. They report that they believe that their children are safe. Catholic religious practice is a durable strength for Mr. Manheim. It prevents him from violent acting out against himself or others, and spiritual community life has elements of intrinsically therapeutic positive psychology from which he benefits. Mr. Manheim was traumatized when his wife was sexually assaulted in March 2015. His trauma became complex when his son Michael was mauled to death by grizzly bears in November 2015. The durable shock of these traumas appears to have driven symptoms of depression and anxiety. Understandably, Mr. Manheim's work—which was a source of pride for him—suffered. At the time of this writing he just concluded short-term disability.

Psychometric assessment depicts an unusually distressed man. The MMPI-2 scores indicate depression, a sense of alienation, suspiciousness, anxiety, uncontrollable thoughts, post-traumatic symptoms, marital distress, ruminations, low self-esteem, work problems, and a guarded attitude toward treatment.

Beck inventories indicate severe levels of depression and anxiety. The PSS-I is positive for the presence of formal PTSD with symptomology related to Paula's assault and Michael's death.

Mr. Manheim's mental status is such that he may suffer from brief dissociative episodes to defend against anguish related to Michael's death. His psychological defenses appear exhausted, and he may not be able to defend against recovering upsetting material from the past that he had formerly repressed. Such material may involve sexual abuse from childhood and emotions related to the sexual abuse trauma that impacted his family that drove them to leave Maine.

Mr. Manheim's clinical presentation and psychometrics support Dr. Swanson's diagnostic hypotheses. Both the MMPI-2 and the PSS-I results support PTSD as a formidable mental pathology. Further, cumulative psychosocial stressors such as lawsuits, work issues, and family and marital discord represent stressors to which Mr. Manheim cannot adjust. These stressors drive severe anxiety and depression. He is in obvious clinical distress and impaired in family, social, and occupational functioning. His defenses appear to have collapsed. Dissociative disorder, not otherwise specified, must be ruled out.

Treatment considerations involve the following: Mr. Manheim presents as quite ill. He should be evaluated for medications as soon as possible. He should also undergo a thorough physical evaluation with blood work. Hospitalization is an option to be considered. Residential care in a Catholic mental health facility is also advisable. All efforts should be made to pair Mr. Manheim with a skilled psychiatrist capable of establishing a meaningful, caring rapport (For a man so ill psychiatric medication, not herbs, are the standard of care). Exposure with response prevention is appropriate for his PTSD symptomatology. Grief work will undoubtedly be called for at several points in the therapeutic process. The "talking cure" and letter writing are also likely to help him ameliorate the severity of PTSD symptoms.

For anxiety and depressive symptoms, a variety of treatment options exist. He will benefit from learning basic cognitive behavioral techniques that involve cognitive restructuring, action planning, and solution orientation. Supportive treatment is also likely to be an ongoing, important factor in the therapeutic alliance. It will keep Mr. Manheim engaged in treatment and prevent regression. Ongoing light physical exercise is a form of behavior modification that will decrease his dysphoric tendencies. His spiritual practices like the rosary and spiritual advising are consistent with his beliefs and, if practiced regularly, are likely to reduce the severity of anxiety and mood symptoms. Family therapy may be advisable at some point. Certainly, a marital process is required. Ongoing assessment of the extent to which Mr. Manheim is sexually traumatized from childhood or sexually compulsive at the current time is required. Ongoing assessment of the nature of family discord is required. To address Mr. Manheim's sense of defeat and misery, CBT mastery and pleasure therapy should be implemented and monitored to maximize therapeutic benefit.

From a psychometric and clinical perspective, Mr. Manheim presents as quite ill. He is traumatized and depressed and anxious to the extreme. He may even briefly dissociate. With this in mind, the notion that he could tolerate the stressors associated with even a simple part-time job is preposterous. Within a reasonable degree of psychological certainty, I find that he is Totally Disabled and cannot work for the foreseeable future.

Answering the Referral Questions

c) Dr. Swanson's existing diagnostic hypotheses are accurate. Rule out dissociative disorder not otherwise specified.

d) Mr. Manheim is unable to perform the material and substantial duties of his occupation and presents as Totally Disabled due to the mental disorders mentioned.

Conclusion of Report

Thank you for the opportunity to examine Mr. Manheim and to provide these findings.

Charles L. Zeiders, Psy.D.
Licensed Psychologist

Lingering Thoughts

Calamity can lead to profound suffering and despair. This was certainly Mr. Manheim's experience. Like most people overcome by disasters, he was unprepared and overcome. Unable to cope with the perfidious sexual assault of his wife and the negligence-driven death of his son, he collapsed. He could no longer function normally in his domestic roles, and his job performance plummeted. Forensic testing revealed a man in profound psychological duress from betrayal, trauma, and grief.

To Mr. Manheim's psychologist, I recommended treatment interventions that might stabilize him. To his attorney, I rendered a determination that Mr. Manheim was no longer capable of employment. But I remained intrigued that Mr. Manheim might heal in a depth-oriented psychotherapy conducted with sensitivity to his Catholic faith. This thought lingered in my consciousness. My discussion with the *Journal of Christian Healing* that follows explores this important matter. A depth therapy with this client, incorporating his Catholic faith, while upholding responsible best practices and sound theory, could be genuinely healing.

****

Reflections on This Case
Interview with Dr. Douglas Schoeninger

Dr. Douglas Schoeninger: How might treatment begin?

Dr. Charles Zeiders: First, treatment must ensure Mr. Manheim's safety. Early in the treatment, even fleeting suicidality presents a mortality risk. Because the patient is in crisis and potentially impulsive, the therapist must establish rapport and enter into a safety agreement with the patient.

Schoeninger: Mr. Manheim suffers like Job. Would you recommend psychotropic medication to Job?

Zeiders: Given the profundity of his signs and symptoms, Mr. Manheim remains too ill to benefit from psychotherapy or to move forward in a healing process without a full psychiatric workup and medication, especially antidepressants and anxiolytics (anxiety inhibitors). For poor old Job, I certainly would recommend this type of intervention.

Schoeninger: Before moving to the spiritual aspects of therapy, would you recommend an intervention like Eye Movement Desensitization and Reprocessing (EMDR) for this patient?

Zeiders: Very much so. EMDR is a powerful trauma-busting tool. The psychotherapist would invite Mr. Manheim to recall distressing imagery, ideas, and sensations related to his wife's rape or his son's horrible death. The therapist would then cause Mr. Manheim's eyes to move back and forth while following a protocol. This widely used trauma treatment should lessen the severity of his trauma, including flashbacks, cognitive avoidance, and hyperarousal.

Schoeninger: Presumably, EMDR's mechanism of action is more than merely placebo or mesmerism?

Zeiders: Absolutely. EMDR is widely used and "is now considered evidence-based practice in the treatment of trauma symptoms."[26] Empirical findings indicate its efficacy in lessening PTSD symptoms. A recent pilot study using brain imaging suggests that eye movements, induced when the patient recalls trauma, may functionally disconnect brain arousal centers from recollection centers. The researchers found that "… preliminary results in [our] small sample suggest that making EMs [eye movements] during recall, which is part of the regular EMDR treatment protocol, might reduce activity and connectivity in emotional processing-related areas."[27]

In other words, the patient recalls the traumatic event and finds that it is no longer traumatic. The eyes of his mind can gaze upon the trauma without the distress he felt prior to treatment. Over time, this evidence-based, trauma-busting technique might pull the neurological plug on Mr. Manheim's trauma.

Schoeninger: Can you talk about how cognitive-behavioral therapy adapted to Mr. Manheim's Christian beliefs might represent a best practice for him?

Zeiders: Cognitive-behavioral therapy (CBT) is an evidence-based treatment for depression and other disorders. The therapist coaches the patient to reframe negative assessments of self, world, others, and the future in terms of more positive, realistic, and true reassessments. This treatment is also promising for anxiety and trauma-based disorders. Research shows that when combined with a patient's religious faith, treatment outcomes may be significantly enhanced. Confirming this, the clinician/researcher Michelle Pearce writes:

---

[26] Christopher William Lee and Pim Cuijpers, "A Meta-Analysis of the Contribution of Eye Movements in Processing Emotional Memories," in *Journal of Behavior Therapy and Experimental Psychiatry*, 44(2):231-9. (2013), 231. https://pdfs.semanticscholar.org/bafl/84e8bfcab6b044e46ddecf9de7031b9f95d2.pdf

[27] Kathleen Thomaes, Iris M. Engelhard, Marit Sijbrandij, Danielle C. Cath, and Odile A. Van den Heuvel, "Degrading Traumatic Memories with Eye Movements: A Pilot Functional MRI Study in PTSD," in *European Journal of Psychotraumatology*, 7 (1), 2016, http://dx.doi.org/10.3402/ejpt.v7.31371

A religious identity and worldview are integral aspects of how religious clients think about, experience, respond to, and take action upon their world, which makes for a good chance that their religious faith is a lens through which they view their experience of depression and recovery. If we don't discuss their religious beliefs and worldview, we may be missing vital information and a significant way of improving their physical well-being.[28]

A team of researchers, led by Dr. Everett Worthington at Virginia Commonwealth University, analyzed data from 46 studies on spiritually integrated therapy published before the end of 2009. This review revealed that religious clients receiving spiritually integrated therapies showed more improvement in psychological as well as spiritual outcomes than those who received alternate psychotherapies. When they compared spiritually integrated psychotherapy to the same type of psychotherapy in secular form, clients receiving the spiritually integrated form of therapy had greater improvement in spiritual outcomes and similar improvement on psychological outcomes.[29]

From a four-and-a-half-year study that integrated Christian faith with CBT, Dr. Pearce found that Christian CBT for appropriate clients was as or more effective than secular CBT for Christian patients. Religiously integrated CBT also improved outcomes on indices of gratitude, altruism, and purpose in life.

Despite Mr. Manheim's profound distress, he is likely to benefit from the inclusion of his miraculously intact Catholic faith in the treatment situation. The inclusion of his faith will enhance his outcomes.

Schoeninger: So much of Mr. Manheim's pain involves grief. How would you address that?

---

[28] Michelle Pearce, *Cognitive Behavioral Therapy for Christians with Depression: A Practical Tool-Based Primer* (Conshohocken, PA: Templeton Press; 2016), 3-4.

[29] Everett L. Worthington Jr., Charlotte Van Oyen Witvliet, Pietro Pietrini, and Andrea J. Miller, "Forgiveness, Health, and Well-Being: A Review of Evidence for Emotional Versus Decisional Forgiveness, Dispositional Forgivingness, and Reduced Unforgiveness," *Journal of Behavioral Medicine*, 30 (4), 2007, 291-302, p. 8.

Zeiders: I would conduct psychotherapy based, in part, on the model developed by grief therapist Kathleen O'Hara. She writes from the experience of profound loss. Her son Aaron was murdered while he was in college at Franciscan University in Steubenville, Ohio. Not only is she a skilled psychotherapist, she credibly walked her own journey from trauma and unutterable grief.[30]

Like O'Hara at the beginning of her journey, grief overwhelms Manheim. His wife has been raped by a trusted spiritual advisor. Betrayal necessitates mourning the dead illusion that a "good shepherd" was a blessing to them. His son's unnecessary and untimely death demands that he address near-unaddressable loss. A skilled psychotherapist might walk O'Hara's seven-stage grief journey with him. It would be a long journey.

Schoeninger: Can you get us started on those stages?

Zeiders: Stage 1: Tell the Story.

O'Hara writes, "Our stories tell about a special kind of grief, one we can never be prepared for, … Speaking out helps us gain mastery over our emotions."[31]

Stage 2: Discovering Several Important Qualities.

To heal from grief, O'Hara advises, the survivor must discover the inner resources of courage, hope, faith, optimism, humor, patience, joy, and compassion. Her faith in the afterlife was especially compelling. It created psychological space for a consoling vision of her late son.

In July 1999, two months after Aaron's death, I was sitting on the beach in New Jersey. … I recalled Aaron playing in the sand. I began to cry because he was gone; I couldn't believe his senseless murder had happened. Then I became of aware of someone next to me. I looked; it was Aaron, tall, healthy, tanned, a beautiful vision, unlike the horror of what had happened to him. He said, "Mom, I'm so happy!" I looked at him and cried. … He stayed with me awhile until I felt at peace. While I was

---

[30] Kathleen O'Hara, *A Grief Like No Other: Surviving the Violent Death of Someone You Love* (New York: Marlowe & Company, 2006).

[31] O'Hara, *Grief.*

glad for him, I missed him so much. I wanted him back. Yet, I was comforted by his visit. I was grateful that he was still alive in his own way and most of all that he was happy. Whether this vision is "real" or not is irrelevant. My beliefs gave me a connection with my son in the afterlife and that is what I needed. I have nurtured that belief in the years since his death.[32]

O'Hara notes that dreams and visions of loved ones are gifts of the spirit and profound consolation delivered through the quality of faith.

Stage 3: Establish Resources.

Resources involve others and special behaviors that provide scaffolding in the midst of the grief work. These include family, friends, community groups, and medical professionals. She also recommends prayer, nature, and art as therapeutic activities. Therapy might encourage the patient to join support groups geared toward healing survivors of clergy sexual abuse.

Stage 4: Prepare for Waves of Grief.

Ego consciousness may endure inundations of extreme sorrow, confusion, guilt, "crazy feelings," loneliness, fear, and anger. Survivors benefit from intellectual normalization of these usually intense emotions and specific strategies to contend with them. Journaling, stress-reductive breathing, and mindful endurance represent coping mechanisms for the patient.

Schoeninger: Could repetitive prayer help Mr. Manheim endure the inundations of grief?

Zeiders: Yes. Depending on his relationship to the Virgin Mary, the Rosary might be especially therapeutic to pray while the ship of his ego is buffeted by storms blowing in from dark regions of his bereaved soul. A specifically Roman Catholic depth psychology exists around the Virgin Mary that bears elaborating. It is believed that praying the Seven Sorrows Devotion— one Our Father and seven Hail Marys for each of Mary's Seven Sorrows, daily—connects the sorrowful person with the divine, loving mother of the savior Jesus Christ. Mary's sorrows consist of:

---

[32] O'Hara, *Grief,* 38.

1. The Prophecy of Simeon telling Mary that she would experience deep anguish from her son's future (Luke 2:34-35).
2. The Flight into Egypt to escape the dreaded murder of the child (Matthew 2:13).
3. The Loss of the Child Jesus in the Temple of Jerusalem, which demonstrated the giftedness of the child but also prefigured the pain of his loss (Luke 2:43-45).
4. The Meeting of Mary and Jesus on the Via Dolorosa where she grieved his impending death (Luke 23:27).
5. The Crucifixion of Jesus on Mount Calvary where Mary endured the death of her Son (John 19:25).
6. The Piercing of the Side of Jesus and His Descent from the Cross (Matthew 27:57-59).
7. The Burial of Jesus by Joseph of Arimathea (John 19:40-42).

For a practicing Catholic, crying out to the Mother of the Church, the New Eve represents a resource in heaven to provide strength to withstand emotional intensity related to the feared or real loss of a child. From the viewpoint of depth psychology, connecting with Mary would be very good for this patient. Prior to his devastating traumas, he soldiered on. He was very much "the man." His high-maintenance family had lots of troubles, and he dealt with them manfully over years while cutting meat at the deli and keeping the money flowing.

Now the devastation is upon him, and he can't function. Devotion to Mary would afford him an opportunity to regress shamelessly to the developmental stage of a needy boy from whom his mother asks nothing. She does not ask him to pull himself together or guilt-trip him back to an age-appropriate role. She holds him and values and guards his safety—just as she did with her son Jesus when the lunatic Herod was killing babies all over Palestine. Manheim can trust her. She understands sadness from her own heart's devastations and therefore holds nothing against him. In God's grace, Mary wants to protect "little ones" because they remind her of her son. For Manheim, Marian devotion would be therapeutic on multiple levels.

Schoeninger: Aside from depth psychological reasons, why else might repetitive prayer help this man?

Zeiders: Repetitive prayer tends to reprogram the nervous system. A storm of emotion can be understood neurologically as an explosion in the autonomic nervous system. The fight/flight response erupts, and the body secretes adrenaline and cortisol, chemicals that drive psychosomatic arousal. In Mr. Manheim's case, unending arousal has been psychosomatically devastating. Because cortisol ruins levels of feel-good neurotransmitters like serotonin, we can credibly guess that high cortisol levels have decimated this brain chemical associated with a normal mood. Repetitive prayer like the Rosary can reverse the psychophysiological ravages of overarousal by turning on the relaxation response associated with the parasympathetic nervous system. Another reason to offer the Rosary to this man is to protect not only his psychological heart, but also his physical heart. Anxiety and depression represent an increased risk of heart disease, and praying the Rosary is likely to create physiological conditions consistent with cardiac health.[33]

Schoeninger: What about Stage Five of O'Hara's grief protocol?

Zeiders: Stage Five occurs after the first year of contending with trauma. O'Hara recommends that survivors cultivate acceptance, forgiveness, and gratitude. Acceptance involves acknowledging the unchangeable, lasting nature of the losses. Forgiveness involves jettisoning feelings of anger, hatred, and revenge. Gratitude involves celebrating what good remains—despite loss—in one's posttraumatic world. The new discipline of Positive Psychology associates all three sensibilities with overall well-being, and experts describe gratitude and forgiveness as among "sacred emotions" that are fostered by religious observance.[34]

Schoeninger: Both his wife's rape and the negligence that led to his son's horrific death represent profound trespasses. If Mr. Manheim was in

---

[33] Luciano Bernardi, Peter Sleight, Gabriele Bandinelli, Simone Cencetti, Lamberto Fattorini, Johanna Wdowczyc-Szulc, and Alfonso Lagi, "Effect of Rosary Prayer and Yoga Mantras on Autonomic Cardiovascular Rhythms: Comparative Study," in *British Medical Journal, 323* (7327), 1446.

[34] Robert A. Emmons, "Emotion and Religion," in Raymond F Paloutzian and Crystal L Park (eds.), *Handbook of the Psychology of Religion and Spirituality* Second Edition (New York: Guilford Press, 2014), 235–252.

treatment with you, how would you approach forgiveness in the context of his Catholic faith?

Zeiders: Every time Mr. Manheim attends Mass, he prays the Lord's Prayer, which involves a general forgiveness of those who trespass against him, so the concept that Catholics forgive would not be lost on him. But it would take a great deal of clinical process for him to be ready emotionally to forgive.

Schoeninger: How do you determine emotional readiness to forgive?

Zeiders: Manheim's anger would have to be available to his ego. To the extent that psychotherapy results in access to retributive emotions and willingness to give them to God, then authentic forgiveness can commence. In treatment or with a reliable religious, I would recommend a forgiveness prayer like this one.

> *Holy Trinity, we offer to you the persons*
> *who have done things to us that have hurt us.*
>
> *We offer to you those who have oppressed us, slandered us, rejected us,*
> *ignored us,*
> *misunderstood us, disappointed us, abused us,*
> *lied to us, stolen from us,*
> *physically harmed us, attacked us,*
> *and done things which we cannot say.*
>
> *By their real or imagined offenses,*
> *we have become wounded.*
> *Our thinking has become disordered,*
> *our feelings painful, our bodies sick,*
> *our experience of life a disappointment.*
>
> *We find that we want to hurt them,*
> *and we want you to hurt them.*

Father, in the midst of the hate and rage
we feel toward these people,
we avail ourselves of the great dignity we possess
as creatures made in the Image of God.

Despite our hurt feelings, thoughts, and bodies,
despite the cruel results in us of others' unkindness
towards us,

we freely abandon our Will to Punish
those who have trespassed against us,
and we freely employ our Will to Forgive them.
We yield the doing of justice to You.
Let no one suffer as they have made us to suffer.

And in so pardoning, O Christ,
according to your teaching and example,
we commit a revolutionary act against the world principles of retaliation
and madness.

We become free from the prison of the Will to Punish
and implore the joyfully approving Father and Son

to send the Holy Spirit
to restore to us all healing,
to remove the afflictions inflicted
and with the graceful medicine that is God's very self
to restore in us the human health
which is the Image of God.

This is our offering, O Father
This is our deed, O Christ
This is our hope, O Spirit. Amen.[35]

---

[35] Charles Zeiders, *Wall Street Revolution and Other Poems* (Skiatook, OK: Fisher King Press, 2013), 16-17.

Schoeninger: If Manheim could pray like that and mean it, what would you predict?

Zeiders: Tremendous relief. Quite possibly, he could experience a sensation of unusual lightness for several days or even weeks.

Schoeninger: For Mr. Manheim, would forgiveness be considered an evidence-based treatment?

Zeiders: It could be. Worthington, et. al. reviewed various studies of forgiveness. From the existing research, he observed, "Emotional forgiveness is the replacement of negative, unforgiving emotions with positive other-oriented emotions. Emotional forgiveness involves psychophysiological changes, and it has more direct health and well-being consequences."[36] From the evidence, Worthington's team speculates that emotional forgiveness results in positive changes in both the peripheral and central nervous systems. Mr. Manheim would find the activity of forgiveness consistent with his recognizable Catholic practice, and the therapist would know that the holding environment honors the patient's culturally derived beliefs with a scientifically ratified intervention.

Schoeninger: What is O'Hara's Stage Six?

Zeiders: Finding creativity is part of the healing. O'Hara observes that creativity "is one of the greatest gifts we possess as human beings. ... [C]reativity is an act of life in response to the chaos of violence ... this stage of the journey ... help[s the survivor] recover the energy of life."[37]
    From the point of view of spiritual psychology, creativity involves the imitation of God, drawing something into existence, and finding it good. Applying this to our case, psychotherapy might reengage Mr. Manheim's dormant enjoyment of gardening and monitor the extent to which it is therapeutic.

Schoeninger: Stage Seven?

---

[36] Worthington, et. al., "Forgiveness," 291.
[37] O'Hara, *Grief,* 145-146.

Zeiders: O'Hara remarks that violence destroys a person's expected future and at some point, he must reinvent that future. Mr. Manheim likely anticipated:
- that he would proceed through life as the *pater familias*,
- that he would provide for his family from his deli manager's salary,
- that he would work until retirement age,
- that "good shepherds" represent the clergy of the Catholic Church, and,
- that he would predecease his children.

Now he finds that, due to impairment from grief and trauma:
- he cannot provide leadership for his family,
- that he is incapable of work,
- that he desperately needs disability income,
- that one of the "good shepherds" raped his wife, and,
- that he will outlive at least one of his beloved children.

The future is upon him, and it is not what he expected.

Schoeninger: Regarding a refurbished future, what would you hope for Mr. Manheim?

Zeiders: Psychotherapy with religious people reveals glimpses of grace that are strikingly beautiful. It is not at all beyond comprehension that Mr. Manheim will discover the God-given meaning to the evils that afflicted him, such that he finds a new vocation. Knowing how God calls him into the world, even into the cosmos, will be the definitive component of his future. Broken-hearted patients, like Mr. Manheim, will transform their ruin to resilience when meaning emerges from their brokenness.

Schoeninger: That's an interesting connection: The *meaning* of suffering makes it endurable and even reveals future purpose.

Zeiders: Jung stated the matter well when he wrote:

Suffering that is not understood is hard to bear, while on the other hand, it is often astounding to see how much a person can endure when he understands the why and wherefore. A philosophical or religious view of the world enables him to do this, and such views prove to be, at the very least, psychic methods of healing if not of salvation.[38]

Schoeninger: Jung's assertion that consciously establishing the positive dimension of suffering via religious meaning anticipates the current development in cognitive-behavioral therapy for Christians with depression.

Zeiders: Yes. Although Jung's analytical psychology is primarily a psychology of the unconscious becoming conscious, his contribution certainly has implications for ego psychologies like cognitive-behavioral therapy—in that the ego must ultimately arrange material it receives from dreams and *spiritus mundi,* the spiritual world. Such things must become and are explicit, life-giving ideas.

Schoeninger: The spiritual world reveals itself to the ego from the unconscious. Can you discuss the unique resources of what I will call "the Catholic unconscious" and the implications for Mr. Manheim's healing?

Zeiders: So much of the history of Catholic religious experience involves the eruption of the unconscious into consciousness during extreme—nearly unendurable—situations. Suffering saints suddenly experience game-changing encouragement and gain energy (antidepressant libido) to make the violent world a better place by helping others (vocation).

The *Dictionary of Miracles* is a compendium of such transformative Catholic depth psychological experience. It lists instances of what appear to be the Catholic unconscious becoming conscious during extreme situations in ways that drive a positive psychological process associated with divine help.[39] The literature of antiquity bursts with examples:

(1) St. Concord was condemned by Torquatas, governor of Umbria, to be beaten with clubs and then hung on "the little horse," a kind of rack. As he was led back to prison heavily laden

---

[38] C. G. Jung, quoted in Edward Hoffman (ed.), *The Wisdom of Carl Jung* (New York: Kensington Publishing, 2003), 214.

[39] E. Cobham Brewer, *A Dictionary of Miracles* (Whitefish, MT: Kessinger Publishing, 2006).

with chains on his hands and neck, he sang praises to God on the way. At night, an angel of the Lord stood by him and said, "[F]ear not, beloved one, but play the man; for I am with thee. The God of Israel is thy strength; his rod and His Staff shall comfort thee."[40]

(2) After St. George had been racked on the wheel by order of the emperor Diocletian, the tormentors thought that he was dead. Scoffing, Diocletian said, "George, where now is thy God? Why does he not help thee?" So saying, he left the dungeon and went to the Temple of Apollo to pay his adorations. Scarcely had he passed the prison gate, when a loud peal of thunder was heard, and a voice came from the cloud, saying, "Fear not, O man of God, for I am with thee. Stand fast in the faith, and many shall be brought to the knowledge of God by thy example." Then appeared an angel, who loosed St. George from the wheel, healed his wounds, and bade him proceed without delay to the temple of Apollo to show himself to the emperor. Diocletian could scarcely believe his eyes; but the empress Alexandra and the two chief captains of the imperial guard were converted to the faith, saying, "No other god can deliver after this sort."[41]

(3) St. Lawrence was racked on the *catasta*, a platform on which slaves were bound in which the limbs are drawn back, then pulled out of joint. Romanus, a Roman soldier who witnessed the torture, went up to St. Lawrence and said, "I see a most beautiful young man standing beside thee and wiping off the blood and sweat as they fall from thee in thine agony. It is a blessed angel sent from heaven to comfort thee. There is no God like thy God, and I am resolved that thy God will be my God, and Him only will I serve." When the martyr was taken from the rack, Romanus brought water and was baptized by him.[42]

---

[40] Brewer, *Dictionary,* 10.

[41] Brewer, *Dictionary,* 10 – 11.

[42] Brewer, *Dictionary,* 11.

In each of these situations: the saint suffers in an unendurable situation when out of nowhere, the unconscious erupts with encouraging/energizing resources. The saint finds energy to bless others, despite his immense suffering. Such religious experience comes from the Holy Spirit and transforms victims into saints. Such potential resides in each of us, no less in the anguished soul of Mr. Manheim. The psychotherapist would do well to wait in hope with this patient that the Holy Spirit would touch his soul in a cosmic kindness masterfully designed to bless this understandably aggrieved man.

Schoeninger: The words of Jesus Christ come to mind: "Blessed are those who mourn for they shall be comforted."[43]

Zeiders: Our Lord intends that his people would be comforted. At Pentecost, the Christian festival celebrating the descent of the Holy Spirit on the disciples of Jesus after his Ascension, held on the seventh Sunday after Easter, the church received the Comforter—the Holy Spirit. And it is an article of faith that the Comforter remains among the faithful and ministers to them, treats them, encourages them, and protects them. My hope for Mr. Manheim is that he would be so blessed.

Schoeninger: Sometimes God uses the faithful to heal the faithful. One sees this in charismatic healing relationships, where a person ordained by the Holy Spirit with a healing gift prays for another's needs. To what extent might charismatic healing benefit Mr. Manheim?

Zeiders: If Mr. Manheim has a positive attitude toward the charismatic Catholic approach, he could benefit a great deal. Partnering with the Holy Spirit in a kind of power healing is experientially real. Several years ago, I assembled a team to study psychological and physical healings related to the Third Person of the Trinity. The study surveyed a group of degreed Christian charismatics in health professions. It sought to understand their experience of healing in relation to the Holy Spirit. Much of the qualitative data was beautiful and edifying:

---

[43] Matthew 5:4

In times of intense emotional pain, as I have reached out to God, I have experienced a warm, gentle yet powerful embrace of a loving energy encircling me from inside out and outside in. I could feel this sensation moving through each cell in my being.

I have often experienced ... energy from the laying on of hands or the holding of others .... Recently, right after [a] death of my [parent], I was held by a [young person] ... related to me by marriage. I was amazed at the awareness of energy flow in me and the level of comfort and healing grace I received—as if an angel were sent to me.

After a fall that crushed several vertebrae, I was unable to move. After being in traction and in extreme pain for three days, unbeknownst to me, a group began to pray for me. I became aware of a sensation that began at my feet (a warmth) and slowly moved up my body. It felt as though a quilt or comforter was being pulled up ... suddenly all pain was gone, and I felt complete peace. It wasn't until later that day that I was told that this is when the group was praying for me. That was twenty-five years ago, and I've never had a problem with my back since.[44]

These experiences are reported by a Catholic professional population from the 21st century, not the first century. Charismatic healing thus represents a potential avenue of healing for Mr. Manheim—a means through which a goodness of which he is presently not conscious could surprise him with divinely given sensations and perceptions that offer an invigorating way forward from betrayal and death.

Schoeninger: When introducing your forensic report, you remarked that the calamities that befell Mr. Manheim could fundamentally fracture his faith in the goodness of God. Can you speculate how such a fracture might heal?

---

[44] Charles Zeiders, Audrey Jean-Jacques., Sherira Fernandes, and Douglas W. Schoeninger, "A Christian Healing Energy Study: Statistical, Qualitative, and Factor Analytical Outcomes of a Survey of the Experience of Healing Energy Among a Subgroup of the Association of Christian Therapists," *Journal of Christian Healing*, 29 (1), 1-44. (2013), 20-21. http://drzeiders.com/wp-content/uploads/2015/09/ChristianHealingEnergy.pdf.FINAL_.pdf

Zeiders: Any Christian who suffers will understandably want a credible explanation of their suffering. Answering this question is problematic. If God is all-good and all-powerful, how can evil afflict us—as it afflicted Mr. Manheim? Either God is not all-good and he tolerates evil, or God is not all-powerful and he cannot prevent evil. When treating Christian patients who ask this question, I tell them frankly that I stand in ignorance. But God is neither fragile nor without resources. God can tolerate frank questions and answer them according to our deepest need. Often a synchronicity, a divinely given coincidence, will break the answer into light. Anyone who needs satisfaction in this area should keep knocking. Jesus affirms that the door will be opened.

Schoeninger: To conclude, how does Christ on the cross address the needs of the contemporary suffering Christian?

Zeiders: Cardinal Sarah offers one answer:

> The words of Christ on the cross echo our doubts precisely. At that time he asked the Father: "Lord, why have you abandoned me?" But Jesus's cry is an act of unfailing confidence, to tell God that he relies on him alone. That is not a cry of rebellion but of filial lament. Today too, when we are lost, like the witnesses of the crucifixion, our doubt is still a hope. If we call out to God, it is because we have confidence. Christian doubt is not a moment of despair but another declaration of love.[45]

Less than a week after the execution of Jesus Christ and the destruction of his movement, the dead man was very much alive, and the despair of his friends was transformed to profound enthusiasm. To understand Christian depth psychology is to realize that God's good news changes psychological darkness to light as it erupts from the unconscious on the wings of the Holy Spirit. Wherever Mr. Manheim is now, may he be so blessed.

---

[45] Sarah, *God or Nothing*, 228.

CHAPTER THREE

The Citizen Who Sued the Police and the Political Spiritualties of Otherness

This chapter explores the political spiritually of *otherness* using a forensic report as a point of departure. The case involves police violence against an African-American Muslim mother (the plaintiff) who was assaulted and traumatized after confronting two plainclothes policemen she believed were acting malevolently against her children. I conducted a forensic evaluation exploring the plaintiff's complaint against the officers. In this chapter, I present the case through the prism of the Jungian collective unconscious and Catholic spirituality of social justice. The mother was suing for damages to herself and her daughter.

Introduction

Five years ago, an attorney known for advancing the cause of those abused by police called me. Late one holiday night in the poor section of a city, a Black Muslim mother was assaulted by two plainclothes policemen. She was about to drive her kids to a relative's house and went back into the house to get some things they'd forgotten. She briefly locked the children in her SUV, which was parked on the street outside her home. Through a window, she saw two men trying to get into the vehicle where her children were asleep. The men were wearing hoodies and dressed like neighborhood punks. She called out to them, but they didn't identify themselves. Fearing for her children, she left the house and confronted them. She had every reason to believe they were threatening her kids.

The men beat her viciously and stung her repeatedly with a Taser. From the locked vehicle, the woman's awake 14-year-old daughter looked on in horror. Only after the woman had been savagely subdued did the violent men identify themselves as plainclothes police officers. They charged the injured woman with endangering children, assaulting police, and disorderly conduct. They removed her parental rights. They wrecked her life. But the courageous mother fought back. In multiple court proceedings, she was declared not guilty, and eventually she regained full custody of her children. But the vicious beating and legal terror left the mother and her 14-year-old daughter injured and traumatized .

The plaintiff, Mrs. Tallis, lost her suit for damages. She made it clear to me that she filed the suit motivated by a sense of citizenship—not out of being an "oppressed" minority, either African-American, Muslim, or female. To her, the issue from beginning to end involved her inalienable rights as an American citizen.

As soon as I accepted the case, I began to feel terrible. I endured frightful sensations as though I were submerged in some kind of evil energy. I suspected it was related to the apparent bad faith of the authorities. A Jesuit mentor of mine once remarked, "Wherever power is abused, there you will find the devil." It was a devil of a case, and I worked hard to stay objective and composed.

In addition to the apparent bad faith of the authorities, the other thing that upset me about the case was the way the police abused the plaintiff. It seemed racist and classist. A few miles from the neighborhood where this African-American Muslim mother was beaten is one of the wealthiest suburbs in America. It's unimaginable that police would treat a suburban mother the way they treated this inner-city woman. It's inconceivable that police would dress in hoodies, get curious about sleeping kids in an SUV outside a McMansion, blow off the alarmed inquires of a white, blond, frightened Episcopalian soccer mom, curse at her during a confrontation; then when she tries to defend her children, beat her up, torture her with a Taser in front of her terrified daughter (no doubt attending a Harvard feeder school), and eventually charge her with improbable crimes after removing her parental rights. The idea that a rich, white female would endure that kind of treatment is inconceivable. That it happened to the plaintiff is socially sickening and morally grotesque.

Since 9/11, Western countries have experienced a turn to the right with nationalist movements burgeoning and setting the tone of political discourse and public policy. Immigration to Europe from Syrians fleeing war and Africans exiting failed states has upset the European Union and member states, whose citizens are accustomed to a degree of cultural homogeneity. Fearing that alien people and cultures will displace their traditions, groups have arisen that represent the fearful elements of the national consciousness. Plus, there is the legitimate fear of radicalized citizens and imported terrorism. A culture of distrust has arisen has arisen in the West, one that sees the *other* as less than human, undeserving of hospitality, kindness, and sanctuary.

The American intellectual and linguist Noam Chomsky has expressed dismay at the European Union's lackluster response to legitimately imperiled Middle Eastern and African refugees. Referring to nationalist extremism, he says,

It's very frightening. … France is awful. East Europe is the worst. Hungary is now run by a virtually neo-Nazi party [Jobbik]. You never really saw the racism in Europe in the past, because it was so homogeneous. When everyone is blonde and blue-eyed, you don't see racism. But as soon as there was the beginnings of immigration, it just came out very dramatically. A lot of people are fleeing Africa, which is a complete horror story—largely because of European actions over the centuries. So, they're fleeing to Europe. The first place they go is Italy. Italy has sort of been rescuing people, but they announced recently that they want to stop; they want to hand it over to the European Union. The EU … announced that they're not going to do much. England said they're not going to do anything. So, if hundreds of thousands of people die at sea, it's their problem—fleeing from centuries of European aggression.[46]

The Catholic Church admonished the European nations for not being more open and helpful to the refugees. Pope Francis compared the Mediterranean to a graveyard where the EU watches the refugees drown. In the meantime, the U.S. elected a president who seems intent on blocking immigration from Muslim countries and nations south of the border.

---

[46] N. Haggerty, "An Interview with Noam Chomsky: Oppression is Not a Law of Nature," *Commonweal*. 2015 https:///www.commonwealmagazine.org/interview-noam-chomsky

Chomsky finds that the United States is like Europe in that it is not a good neighbor to people who have been harmed by heavy-handed American political and economic adventures in their countries.

> We're doing the same thing [as the Europeans]. The people who are fleeing Central America—what are they fleeing from? [*Chomsky indicates violence and institutionalized oppression.*] ... They're fleeing from the aftermath of the virtual genocide in the highlands in the early 1980s that the United States supported. And we pick them up at the border and throw them back. Just a couple days ago, there was a Human Rights Watch report condemning the United States for throwing back refugees— women and children. It's a real horror story. ... They come to the border, and we put them in trucks and send them back to Mexico to die. ... It's pretty shocking.[47]

The United States is turning away people who flee a well-founded fear of persecution—often from economic and political oppression fostered by U.S. meddling in the national affairs of the fleeing individuals. Taking advantage of the culture of fear among alienated segments of the American electorate, the sitting president infamously proposes building a wall to prevent immigration. Labeling refugees as rapists and drug addicts who will steal jobs from Americans, he criminalizes and scapegoats them. The pope weighed in:

> Speaking at his weekly general audience, Francis spoke of a Christian calling "to not raise walls but bridges, to not respond to evil with evil, to overcome evil with good."

> He then improvised and added: "A Christian can never say 'I'll make you pay for that'. Never! That is not a Christian gesture. An offense is overcome with forgiveness, by living in peace with everyone."

---

[47] Haggerty, Interview with Chomsky.

Last year, in response to an answer about then-candidate Trump's views on immigration and his intention to build a wall on the border with Mexico, Francis said a man with those views is "not Christian."

He said in an interview that he would not form an opinion of Trump until he first had a chance to see specific policies the new US president would implement.

As Trump was taking office on Jan. 20, [2017] Francis sent a message urging him to be guided by ethical values, saying he must take care of the poor and the outcast during his time in office.[48]

Certain elements in Europe and the United States tend to scapegoat both external and internal others. This has given rise to movements like Black Lives Matter and United We Dream in the U.S.

Francis calls out the socio-political phenomenon of scapegoating for what it is: a false and inhuman strategy to solve social problems, problems in group behavior and consciousness.

"Scapegoats are not only sought to pay, with their freedom and with their life, for all social ills such as was typical in primitive societies, but over and beyond this, there is at times a tendency to deliberately fabricate enemies: stereotyped figures who represent all the characteristics that society perceives or interprets as threatening," he said. "The mechanisms that form these images are the same that allowed the spread of racist ideas in their time."

This is the closest Francis came to addressing the Black Lives Matter movement before his visit to the U.S. in September 2015. Like many activists in the [Black Lives Matter] movement, Francis suggests that racial scapegoating factors into why society

---

[48] P. Pullella. "Don't Build Walls, Pope says," Reuters. https://af.reuters.com/article/worldNews/ idAFKBN15N1ZZ, May 15, 2017

favors taking freedom away from some groups and placing them behind bars for years rather than remedy the social ills that keep prisons overflowing.[49]

Pope Francis is assuming a prophetic role in a Western world that has drifted to the right. He is, essentially, the shadow, in Jungian terms, of regressive extremism. This pope offers a perennial spirituality that recognizes the dignity of every man and woman. The test of whether a social attitude or public policy is pestilential or perennial is whether the dignity and rights of the other is upheld. For Francis, this attitude is predicated on the Catholic teaching that God creates each human being is his image. This Christian idea—abstracted into deism by Thomas Jefferson—resonates with the best of American political spiritual anthropology, which states in the Declaration of Independence:

We hold these truths to be self-evident, that all men are created equal, that they are endowed by their Creator with certain unalienable Rights, that among these are Life, Liberty and the pursuit of Happiness.

Forensic Psychological Report [blinded]

Subjects: Cecilia Tallis and Bridget Tallis
Evaluator: Charles Zeiders, PsyD, Licensed Psychologist
Date of report: 10/9/13

Sources of information
Letter from Frank Dowd, Esq., 9/22/13;
Oral Deposition of Cecilia Tallis, 5/21/13;
Oral Deposition of Bridget Tallis, 5/21/13;
Document listed as Case 2:12-cv-05444-PBT, filed 10/9/12;
Medical Records of Metropolitan Counseling Professionals for Cecilia Tallis covering treatment interval from 1/5/12 to 5/6/13;

---

[49] N. Nittle, "Five Quotes from Pope Francis on Racism, Xenophobia, and Immigration," ThoughtCo. https://www.thoughtco.com/pope-francis-on-racism-xenophobia-and-immigration-2834555 , May 15, 2017

Medical Records of Metropolitan Counseling Professionals for Bridget Tallis covering treatment interval from 3/8/12 to 3/3/13.

Letter from Peter Carrol, LCSW containing treatment summary for Cecilia Tallis, 7/26/13;

Letter from Thomas Prust, MD & Catherine T. Dunphy, MA containing treatment summary for Bridget Tallis, 7/13/13

Corroboration from third parties:

George Taylor: father of Cecilia; grandfather of Bridget; spoke via phone approximately 15 minutes on 10/8/13;

Amanda Beckett: friend of Cecilia; spoke via phone approximately 15 minutes on 10/8/13;

Claire Case; friend of family; spoke via phone approximately 15 minutes on 10/8/13.

Clinical Methods

Clinical interview with Cecilia Tallis on 10/7/13 which included interview for PTSD pegged directly to DSM-IV symptoms for PTSD, 5 pm – 7 pm;

Clinical interview with Bridget Tallis on 10/7/13 which included interview for PTSD pegged directly to DSM-IV symptoms for PTSD, 7 pm – 8:15 pm;

Intake Information template complete by both subjects;

Depression Checklist completed by both subjects;

PTSD Checklist (PCL-S), Beck Depression Inventory-II, Beck Anxiety Inventory (Cecilia only)

Identification of the subjects

Cecilia Tallis, born 4/12/77, resides in a major metropolitan city. She lives with her husband Robert and her 6 children, ranging in age from 4 months to 14. She has been married for 16 years and her chief occupation is caring for her family. Their oldest daughter, Bridget, born 11/06/98, resides with her parents and is also a subject of this report. Both subjects are embedded in an extended family network that is reasonably strong. They practice Islam.

Circumstances of referral and referral question
This psychology practice was contacted by Frank Dowd, Esquire, of The Dowd Firm, who represents the subjects in Tallis et al v. Community Policing, et al. The referral question involved substantiating whether the subjects credibly displayed post-traumatic symptomatology following a traumatic encounter with Police Officers from the Community Policing Department.

History of precipitating event
On November 27, 2010, Cecilia Tallis was in the midst of celebrating the Thanksgiving Holiday. Taking her children from one family event to another, she parked her car full of sleeping children in front of her residence on or about 12:45 a.m. Cecilia locked the car and told her eldest child, Bridget, who was awake, of her intention to grab a suitcase from the house and return immediately to the vehicle. She then entered the residence. A moment later, Cecilia saw from a window a stranger attempting to open the door of the vehicle where she had safely locked Bridget and her four siblings.

Bridget felt frightened, because the stranger knocked on the vehicle door without identifying himself.

From her vantage in the residence, Cecilia also saw that a strange truck had appeared and blocked the vehicle that contained her children. Thinking that her children were in danger, she exchanged words with the stranger from the window and left the house to protect her children from someone she thought might be a bad actor.

On the street, Cecilia told the man to get away from her children. He responded by pushing her against a metal fence. He then choked her and lifted her off the ground. She found it difficult to breathe. At that point, the actor identified himself as a police officer.

Then, with another police officer, also in plainclothes, the two men continued to forcefully handle Cecilia. They threw her face down in the grass. One man put his knee or foot on the back of her neck and the other held her as she was handcuffed.

During this time neighbors were yelling to the men to leave Cecilia alone. Bridget also yelled to the men to stop beating up her mother.

More officers arrived. Cecilia was tased repeatedly while handcuffed. Bridget witnessed this treatment of her mother; she witnessed sparks flying from the tasers applied to Cecilia's body, and was mentally disturbed by what she saw.

In between tasings, Cecilia yelled out to her neighbor to call her spouse and yelled to Bridget to call her grandfather. Bridget recalled that every time Cecilia yelled a phone number to the neighbor, another tase was applied to her mother's prone, helpless body.

Eventually, the police took Cecilia into custody and charged her with endangering the welfare of children, resisting arrest, and disorderly conduct. She was found not guilty on both charges. Despite the judicial outcomes in her favor, the experience took a toll on Cecilia and Bridget. The frightful events described caused mother and daughter to develop mental health problems.

History of symptoms, diagnoses, and treatments
By the time Cecilia was found not guilty of her second charge, her family felt concerned for her. She demonstrated symptoms of loss of interest in matters that used to engage her; she evidenced self-isolation, irritability, sleep problems, and a variety of post-traumatic symptoms.

She entered treatment with Metropolitan Counseling Professionals. In a May 23, 2012, Comprehensive Treatment Plan, Cecilia's therapist, Paige Johnson, MCC, listed Cecilia's primary diagnosis as Post-Traumatic Stress Disorder (PTSD), because Cecilia's symptoms included flashbacks and nightmares about the November 27, 2010, incident with the police.

In a June 27, 2013, treatment summary, Peter Carrol, LCSW, noted:

Ms. Cecilia Tallis was given a provisional diagnosis of Post-Traumatic Stress Disorder by Paige Johnson on May 23, 2012, based on reported symptoms of flashbacks and nightmares of incident with police, anxiety, poor appetite, isolation, insomnia, and anger, loss of interest in activities, reduced energy and concentration.

Please note that a provisional diagnosis may change depending on the findings\assessment from the psychiatrist who gives a final diagnosis.

On June 11, 2013, Cecilia's psychiatrist diagnosed her with Depressive Disorder, Not Otherwise Specified, because Cecilia presented with symptoms of isolation, sleep problems, appetitive problems, fatigue, lack of concentration, loss of interest, and anxiety. It should be noted that symptoms of depression often accompany symptoms of post-traumatic stress.

Cecilia missed scheduled psychiatric evaluation appointments on July 10 and October 9, 2012. She credibly attributes these missed appointments to her duties as a busy mother of six children.

During a November 20, 2012, medication management appointment with a Dr. Smryna, Cecilia's medication (which had been prescribed to treat agitation and sleep problems associated with the hyperarousal and anxious depression associated with post-traumatic symptomatology) was discontinued, because Cecilia was pregnant and there was concern for the health of the fetus.

In addition to psychiatric treatment, Cecilia also received fourteen individual psychotherapy treatments. These occurred with the interval between January 1, 2012, and May 6, 2013. She continues to try to attend treatment once a month. These sessions address Cecilia's post-traumatic and mood symptoms.

In her deposition testimony, Cecilia admits to experiencing durable symptoms of post-traumatic stress in the form of ongoing nightmares about the November 27, 2010, incident with the police and a reaction of emotional discomfort when she sees law enforcement officers.

Like her mother, Bridget also suffered mental distress from the incident. During her deposition, she remarked that she went into mental health treatment, "Because I was like having nightmares ever since it [the November 27, 2010, incident] happened and my behavior in school acted up."

Prior to the frightening incident, she evidenced no behavioral problems. She further remarked, "I used to have flashbacks of what happened. And like it wasn't like good nightmares, it was like very bad ones, and I used to wake up crying every time."

From her May 8, 2012, initial evaluation at Metropolitan Counseling Professionals (MCP), Bridget was diagnosed with an Adjustment Disorder, but following a psychiatric evaluation conducted by Dr. Thomas Prust, Bridget's diagnosis was changed to Post-Traumatic Stress Disorder.

In a July 13, 2013, letter cosigned by Bridget's counselor and psychiatrist, Catherine Dunphy, MA, and Thomas Prust, MD respectively, it was documented that following Dr. Prust's psychiatric evaluation, Bridget's diagnosis of Post-Traumatic Stress Disorder was justified, because she met the official diagnostic criteria at the time. In a treatment summary contained in that same document, the counselor and psychiatrist wrote:

> Bridget Tallis' gross behavior difficulty dates back to the age she witnessed her mother being badly beaten by police officers. Following this incident, Bridget began to isolate herself and stopped interacting with friends. She became angry, defiant, oppositional, and was talking back to adult authority figures. Bridget stated during evaluation, that the worst thing that ever happened to her was "seeing my mother beaten by police." Bridget's symptoms included hypersomnolence, anxiety, anger, crying/sadness, and flashbacks.

In his June 6, 2012, psychiatric evaluation of Bridget, Dr. Prust noted that Bridget's PTSD was "resolving."

From her March 8, 2012, admission until her March 3, 2013, discharge, Bridget attended eleven individual or group treatment sessions.

In her May 21, 2013, deposition testimony, Bridget noted that her nightmares had subsided but that exposure to the police continued to make her concerned that she is in a dangerous presence.

Third party corroboration and observation

To understand Cecilia and Bridget's pre- and post-trauma functioning, the evaluation process involved gathering corroboration and observation information from third parties familiar with the subjects. All conversations occurred the morning of October 8, 2013, and each lasted approximately fifteen minutes.

George Taylor identified himself as father to Cecilia and grandfather to Bridget. He works as an environmental engineer for Metropolitan Environmental Protection. He remarked that Cecilia's development, prior to the November 27, 2010, incident with the police was characterized by normalcy and happiness. He noted that Cecilia and Bridget were part of an extended family whose traditions preclude drug and alcohol use. He described Cecilia as a "goody two shoes" and that irresponsible or criminal behavior were completely foreign to her. He reported that through her developmental stages, Cecilia demonstrated an outgoing, fun-loving nature. She went to a high school dedicated to the performing arts. She played the piano and liked to sing. She attended classes two years at the Metropolitan Performing Arts Academy, prior to starting her family and dedicating herself to her children while assisting her husband in a business that involved child entertainment. He noted that prior to the incident with police, Cecilia was pleasant, outgoing, social, open, and extroverted. Immediately after, she "was the converse." To Mr. Taylor, his daughter had become morose, withdrawn, less social, closed, and isolative. She appeared to lose her zest for life, often appeared agitated, and presented as more irritable than her previous self. Also, "she was angry at the injustice of the matter." He noted that she miscarried after the incident and that she felt tormented by the possibility that the traumatic incident with the police may have played a role in the loss of her child. He also described her as more easily agitated after the incident with the police. To him, Cecilia appears more vulnerable to the stresses of life. He sees Cecilia and his grandchildren "about every weekend." He noted that more recently Cecilia appears less unhappy than in the year immediately following the accident but that she is not back to her old self.

Mr. Taylor noted how he observed Bridget prior to the incident with the police. She was "like her mother, outgoing and affable. Now she presents as more subdued" and has "a less positive demeanor." In the year following the incident, Bridget appeared less engaged in life to her grandfather. She appeared angry and upset from witnessing the behavior of the police. Mr. Taylor believes that Bridget has less confidence in authorities, especially the police.

Amanda Beckett identified herself as a friend of Cecilia's for twenty years. Ms. Beckett is a Teacher's Assistant at Metropolitan County College. Ms. Beckett described Cecilia as a loving mother who experienced the incident with the police as "a traumatic experience" for Cecilia. She further remarked, "I was really shocked by the charges of child neglect, because she has always been a caring, attentive, and giving mother." Ms. Beckett noted that she finds Cecilia to be "honest and truthful," a caring person, and feels comfortable entrusting her own daughter to Cecilia's care. In the year following the incident, Ms. Beckett visited Cecilia to support her and still remains in twice-monthly phone contact. Ms. Beckett believes that the traumatic incident has made Cecilia more protective of her children and less secure about their safety. She did not feel that she knew Bridget well enough to opine.

Claire Case identified herself a family friend of eighteen years. She lives in the same major metropolitan city, and Cecilia calls her daily and visits once a week. Ms. Case notes that in the year prior to the incident with the police, Cecilia was outgoing and family-oriented. She was friendly and eager to help others and "always happy." In the year following the incident, Cecilia presented as very withdrawn. "She didn't seem like herself." Ms. Case described Cecilia as becoming "very careful" with her children and less trusting of others and the police. Ms. Case notes that Cecilia is still "not as relaxed as she used to be." She noted that she is glad Cecilia enjoys ongoing family support.

Ms. Case further noted that in the year prior to the incident, Bridget was "sweet and sensitive "and a typical kid." She described Bridget as "nice and respectful." After the incident, she saw Bridget change. She observed Bridget become upset and cry when exposed to material on television that involved assault plots. She believes that Bridget became protective of her mother and would "check on her mother to see how" Cecilia was doing.

While subject to some level of bias due to the fact that the above reporters know and are loyal to Cecilia and Bridget, their third-party corroboration regarding mental status prior and after an experience of mental injury is considered a reasonable and customary way to gather information for an examination of this sort. One authoritative tome remarks "… third party information is a mandatory component of most forensic evaluations."[50]

The reporters corroborate that following the incident with the police they observed a marked change in the subjects' presentation. These informal but important observations depict both subjects as being deleteriously impacted by the traumatic incident with the police. Further, the remarks of these reporters offer information about the changes in the subjects that are consistent with observations of the mental health providers of MCP who documented symptoms of PTSD and depression in both subjects. None of the above reporters expressed partisan antipathy for the police, but all of them expressed knowledge and concern for the subjects' mental welfare.

Psychological examination

On October 7, 2013, Cecilia and Bridget Tallis came to my office for psychological examination. Both completed and Intake Information From, and a Depression Checklist. Cecilia was further administered the PTSD Checklist (PCL-S), Beck Depression Inventory-II, and Beck Anxiety Inventory—all relevant measures of PTSD, depression, and anxiety, respectively, and normed on adults. These instruments possess psychometric properties and are generally accepted by psychologists as screening measures to establish the presence of symptoms of mental

---

[50] Melton, et al. 2007, p 53.

disorders. Because the subjects' mental injuries were sustained and diagnosed by MCP under the DSM-IV-TR diagnostic system [*Diagnostic and Statistical Manual of Mental Disorders*, Fourth Edition, Text Revision], the clinical interview for PTSD and related symptomatology was pegged to that same diagnostic system.

Examination of Cecilia Tallis

Cecilia was informed of the purpose of the examination and consented to it for herself and her daughter. She identified herself as thirty-six-year-old female living in a major metropolitan city with her husband and 6 children. She listed her presenting problem as: "dealing with the traumatic life change I was put through as a result of being beaten by male police officers causing the loss of my baby." She noted that she was still "suffering mentally, physically, emotionally." She noted that she last saw her physician in 2012, when she was pregnant with her now four-month-old daughter. She reported that she had resumed mental health treatment at MCP with a Mr. Costa and that she had resumed taking medication.

The PTSD examination offered the following information about her symptoms in relation to DSM-IV-TR criteria for that disorder. She met Criteria A: She experienced the incident with the police as a traumatic event in that she feared for her own safety and the safety of her children. She also felt afraid and helpless. She met Criteria B: She re-experienced the traumatic event in one or more ways. She noted that when off her medication, during her last pregnancy, television would trigger distressing recollections of the event; she also reported nightmares about the event. She further re-experienced the event in the form of an emotionally upsetting anniversary reaction to the trauma last Thanksgiving; this was confirmed in her MCP treatment file; the holiday was an external cue that symbolized the traumatic event. She met Criteria C: She has evidenced persistent avoidance of stimuli associated with the trauma and numbing of general responsiveness not present before the trauma as indicated by three or more symptoms: She affirms that she tries to avoid thoughts and feelings related to the incident with the police. She also experienced a diminished participation with her own family and other families with children. She also admitted to the symptom of feeling detached and estranged from others; at times, she has isolated herself. She met Criteria

D: She affirms persistent symptoms for increased arousal, not present before the trauma, as indicated by two or more symptoms. She has difficulty falling asleep and she has difficulty staying asleep. She is positive for the symptom of hypervigilance, and for example, is overly alert when getting in and out of her car with her children. After the trauma, she developed an exaggerated startle response. She met Criteria E: Her symptoms have existed on and off since the trauma of November 27, 2010, were witnessed by treatment providers at MCP, and were further reported to have been present in the month leading up to the interview. She met Criteria F: Cecilia's disturbance causes clinically significant distress as evidenced by the subject crying during the interview and reporting suffering from her symptoms; her symptoms also impair her participation in the important areas of family life and the family business. Her PTSD is specified as "chronic," because the duration of her symptoms is three months or longer.

Other findings of the examinations are that she scored in the clinical range on the PTSD Checklist (PCL-S); on this instrument, she endorsed symptoms of PTSD in a manner similar to responses during the clinical interview; she was positive for experiencing the necessary number of symptoms of PTSD in the past month to qualify for that diagnosis using this instrument. Her severity score was 55, which is considered a high score on this instrument. The test was administered to this subject strictly according to the administration instructions. Her Beck Anxiety Inventory score of 15 was at the very top of the mild range and just below the moderate range. Her Beck Depression Inventory-II yielded a score of 28 in the moderate depression range. She endorsed enough symptoms on the Major Depressive Disorder Checklist to credibly qualify for a Depressive Disorder.

Mental status: Cecilia came to my office forty-five minutes early with her daughter Bridget and her baby Jack. She was polite, cooperative, and appropriately dressed. During the interview, her affect ranged from pleasant during our preliminary conversation, to hurt sadness and fear when describing the trauma. When she disclosed her concern that her miscarriage may have been related to the traumatic experience of November 17, 2010, her face displayed a look of inconsolable anguish. She made it clear that her symptoms did not impair her ability to love her children or care for them. She demonstrated insight by saying that the traumatic incident with the police robbed her of a certain zest she used to bring to her vocation as a mother. Her resumption of mental health treatment combined with psychiatric care may help her regain that zest. She also disclosed, with a look of sadness and hurt, that she felt burdened by the fact that she was charged with crimes when she thought she was protecting her children. She became very distressed and cried briefly when reviewing the traumatic incident. She presented with normal concentration during the interview but noted that often her concentration is poor in her daily life. There was no evidence of a thought disorder and a denial of suicidal ideation.

Diagnosis
Axis I: 309.81 Posttraumatic Stress Disorder, Chronic
   311 Depressive Disorder, NOS
Axis II: 799.9 Diagnosis Deferred
Axis III: None reported
Axis IV: Litigation; birth of a child in large family
Axis V: 60

Examination of Bridget Tallis

Following Cecilia's examination, Bridget was examined. Her mother sat in the waiting room and the door to the office was left slightly ajar. Bridget was told that she could leave the examination at any time if she became uncomfortable. A white-noise machine was whirling outside the office door, however, so that the conversation in the examining room did not reach the waiting room. When asked if she was coached in any way to answer questions in a specific manner, Bridget noted that her mother told her simply to tell the truth.

Bridget's PTSD examination offered the following information about her symptoms in relation to DSM-IV-TR criteria for that disorder. She met Criteria A: She experienced the incident with the police as a traumatic event and feared for her mother's safety. During the incident, she felt intense fear. She met Criteria B: She re-experienced the traumatic event in one or more ways. She noted that she re-experienced the trauma in nightmares about the event, and these concluded sometime in 2011. She did not formally meet all of Criteria C: Bridget was positive for two avoidance symptoms, as opposed to the three symptoms required. Bridget reported that she tries to avoid thinking about the event, because thinking about the event is upsetting. She has avoided returning to places that remind her of the trauma; specifically, she noted that she has refused invitations to return to the neighborhood in which the incident with the police occurred. (Another interviewer or questioning style might have elicited a third symptom.) She met Criteria D: She affirms persistent symptoms for increased arousal not present before the trauma and indicated by two or more symptoms. She experienced insomnia for up to two months after the event and has experienced sleep issues on and off since, depending on psychosocial stressors. She believes that the trauma has increased her irritability. She also finds that she is jumpier in general, indicative of an exaggerated startle response. She noted that seeing grown men, especially policemen, drives her startle response. She met Criteria E: By history, the duration of Bridget's symptoms has been more than one month. She met Criteria F: The disturbance causes clinically significant distress as evidenced by problems with authority figures and deep inner pain. If she were to be diagnosed with PTSD, the specifier would be "chronic," because the duration of her symptoms is three months or longer.

Bridget qualified for all the criteria of PTSD, minus one symptom under Criteria C. From a diagnostic point of view, Bridget presents as a traumatized young woman who has suffered most of the formal symptoms of PTSD since the incident with the police. Examination at a later time might reveal a complete diagnostic qualification for PTSD. Dr. Prust, Bridget's psychiatrist and diagnostician at MCP, credibly provided a full PTSD diagnosis when Bridget was under his care.

During the examination, Bridget made several important disclosures, and we talked about them. She noted that she did not think that her previous treatments ameliorated her distress. She indicated that an effective rapport may have been lacking with the previous psychotherapist. She also disclosed she does not believe that she has told anybody the full story of what is occurring in her mind and emotions about the November 27, 2010, incident with the police. She said that she still suffers and feels upset from witnessing her mother's beating. She disclosed that these thoughts and feelings remain "all locked up." She painted a picture of herself as deeply and traumatically affected by the incident with the police with cognitions and emotions about the matter under-processed and under-disclosed. She also talked about experiencing passive suicidal ideation, that is, she does not intend to kill herself but feels so much distress that the idea of dying is more welcome than frightening. (At the conclusion of treatment, I advised Bridget's concerned mother about this. Cecilia agreed to get Bridget back into treatment. She wrote down the names of several groups that I recommended could help this distressed adolescent immediately.) Bridget seemed eager to discuss how distressed she felt, and she insightfully noted that she was contending both with "trauma stuff" and "teenage stuff." Trauma often complicates development.

Bridget endorsed enough symptoms on the Major Depressive Disorder Checklist to credibly qualify for a Depressive Disorder. She indicated that her feelings of depression were for more than two weeks and began in 2013. Symptoms she endorsed involved a depressed mood, diminished interest, early-morning insomnia, feelings of worthlessness (from issues with her peer group), diminished concentration, and passive suicidality.

Mental Status: Bridget presented with anxious and frightened affects and a depressed mood. She seemed eager to disclose the level of her distress. She had insight into the fact that she had not processed or disclosed the entire trauma that she sustained from witnessing the beating of her mother. She further had insight that the psychosocial stress of embroilment in the legal system was very hard on her. She conveyed insight that she recognizes a distinction between developmental problems of being a teenager and issues more discretely related to the traumatic experience she underwent with her mother. She noted that members of her extended family make her feel both safe and comforted. She displayed no symptoms of a thought disorder. She appeared relieved to have disclosed her depressive symptoms, including her passive suicidality, and to be back on her way into treatment.

Axis I: R/O Post-Traumatic Stress Disorder
  R/O Anxiety Disorder NOS

311 Depressive Disorder NOS
Axis II 799.9 No Diagnosis
Axis III: Headaches (by previous history)
Axis IV: litigation; stress from school and peers
Axis V: 50

Answering the referral question

Cecilia and Bridget Tallis experienced the November 27, 2010, event with the police as traumatic and developed symptomatology consistent with Post-Traumatic Stress Disorder. PTSD was the dominant diagnostic hypothesis for both Cecilia and Bridget as they underwent treatment at MCP. Cecilia's PTSD diagnosis was provisional; Bridget's was formal. Third parties corroborate that the incident with the police appeared to disrupt the lives of both subjects. This evaluation offers diagnostic conclusions similar to those reached by MCP diagnosticians. Both subjects present with a diagnostic picture of PTSD or a symptom profile almost identical to PTSD. Both subjects present with symptoms of major depression which often accompanies post-traumatic stress. According to Cecilia and Bridget, their MCP providers, and third parties, their symptoms emerged from the traumatic incident with police on November 27, 2010. From a mental health perspective, that incident with the police was a calamity for both subjects. That calamity caused and drove post-traumatic and mood symptoms in both subjects. I offer these opinions with a reasonable degree of psychological certainty.

****

Reflections on This Case
Interview with Dr. Douglas Schoeninger

Dr. Douglas Schoeninger: From the viewpoint of depth psychology, what do you make of the violence that the police inflicted upon these traumatized women?

Dr. Charles Zeiders: In the current stage of the evolution of consciousness, police inhabit a power archetype. This is necessary for them to protect society. No matter what, society needs defense mechanisms. But the Western world now suffers a degradation of mass consciousness. In this context police power tends toward not public protection but public domination—of social elements considered *other* by the establishment.

> Even in modern democracies, police who harm or kill civilians are rarely sanctioned by their superiors, very rarely indicted, and hardly ever convicted. ... In American culture, violence against criminals and suspects is integral to the authority of the police. ... Police forces train officers in the use of violence, which is taken for granted as natural, necessary, and morally salutary. Violence is a potential means of ... [controlling] ... anyone stopped by the police; the threat is evident in the guns and clubs carried by police officers, along with the knowledge that police are rarely convicted of assault or homicide against anyone they apprehend. ... Police also feel that violence enhances respect for their authority ...[51]

Schoeninger: You're saying that police violence against the other is part of a mass defense mechanism?

Zeiders: Yes. And we can learn about the chief defensive project of any society—any mass consciousness—by studying the impact of the leaders the society allows to reach power. The current U.S. president fuels a mass scapegoating phenomenon; he legitimizes locating evil in the Other, and this is an expression of regression within the American psyche. It actively departs from the political anthropology offered in the Declaration of Independence that all are created equal; it disturbingly discards the spiritual dimension of the human rights of the so-called Other, whose inalienable rights must be respected by the state, because God makes this demand upon the state. Since the Creator endows each living person with rights, no government can trespass against a person without defying God and natural law.

---

[51] A. Fiske and T. Rai, Virtuous Violence. New York: Cambridge University Press, 2015), 49.

Schoeninger: It's easy to imagine that—should the state persist in its expression of defensive consciousness—then elements of the Other might resort to violence and revolution for self-protection, or even healing.

Zeiders: That's a good point. Here is one sad example among many: After the Second World War, the charismatic black French psychiatrist Frantz Fanon hypothesized that the French imperial violence inflicted upon colonial Algeria wrought mental illness upon the Algerian population. For the radical psychiatrist, bloody revolution against the French oppressor amounted to mass psychiatric self-treatment.

> Fanon described how violence could serve as a cleansing force for the colonized, liberating them not only from their colonial masters but from their inferiority complex. ... [Revolutionary violence] ... was a rite of passage for colonized communities and individuals who had become mentally ill ... as a result of the settler-colonial project, itself saturated with violence and racism.[52]

> The questions Fanon raised about the limits of Western humanism, and the barriers separating the rich and the poor worlds, are still pertinent today. The boundaries that separate the West from the rest, and from its internal others, have been redrawn since his death, but they have not disappeared. The coercive unveiling of Muslim women has reappeared in France. ... In the US, the killings of unarmed black people by the police have furnished a grim new genre of reality television, and a reminder of the vulnerability of the black body. The president ... has surrounded himself with avowed white supremacists. The cities of the liberal West, with their slums and gated enclaves, are nearly as compartmentalized as colonial Algiers ...[53]

---

[52] A. Shatz, "Where Life Is Seized," *London Review of Books.* January 19, 2017, 19.

[53] Shatz, "Where Life Is Seized," 27.

Schoeninger: Fanon's focus is a secular example of revolution against oppression. Can you offer an example of revolution against oppression that is spiritually inspired?

Zeiders: Nat Turner's visionary experience is an example of this. Whenever the other finds itself unable to redress society's structural sins, exploitation, and entrenched mass scapegoating, the collective unconscious will eventually erupt into the psyche of a "messianic" leader; this leader will endure dreams and visions of an apocalyptic nature; the leader will emerge from the visionary experience convinced that Almighty God commands them to free the oppressed. In Nat Turner's case, he saw visions and heard a voice that inspired him to lead a frightful, pre-Civil War slave rebellion in the U.S. Prior to his hanging, Turner told an interviewer:

> I heard a loud noise in the heavens, and the Spirit instantly appeared to me and said the Serpent [which represented the slave holding establishment] was loosened, and Christ had laid down the yoke he had borne for the sins of men, and that I should take it on and fight against the Serpent, for the time was fast approaching when the first should be last and the last should be first. ... And by signs in the heavens ... I should arise and prepare myself and slay my enemies with their own weapons.[54]

During the doomed rebellion, Turner ordered fellow slaves to slaughter any person whomsoever they believed benefited from the institution of slavery. In doing this, Turner and his followers believed that they were fulfilling the commandments of God to set the people free.

It is clear that Nat Turner felt that he was being obedient to the will of God .... when he led the bloody insurrection of 1831. Of course, this raises the question of whether obedience which leads to such actions is really the will of God or whether it is merely the whim of man who finds himself in a situation of oppression. Whatever we might think, Nat Turner was assured that his violent expression against the oppressors evolved out of

---

[54] K. Greenberg, ed., *The Confessions of Nat Turner and Related Documents* (New York: St. Martin's Press, 1996), 47-48.

the will of God. ... And the Old Testament is filled with incidents in which rebellion by the oppressed was seen as fulfilling the will of God; and in the New Testament, in a moment of disgust in the synagogue, Jesus himself used a whip to teach a lesson ...[55]

Schoeninger: Can the messianic mission of such a salvation figure stem from nonviolent spiritual inspiration?

Zeiders: Very much. Martin Luther King and then later Malcolm X are wonderful exemplars of this. Pope Francis urges the leaders of the Western world to set the tone in upholding the dignity of minority citizens and aliens desperate for asylum. If this could be achieved, apocalyptic radicalization would be less of a threat. Even the germ of apocalyptic radicalization would diminish. This could be especially true for black and Muslim persons.[56]

Schoeninger: To what extent do you believe that scapegoating and Islamophobia played a role in the mistreatment of the woman in your report?

Zeiders: A bit. According to the Council on American-Islamic Relations, the status of Muslim civil rights in the U.S. has suffered in recent years.

> After 9/11 ..., there was a violent backlash against some American Muslims ... some Americans who merely looked Muslim have been victims of various forms of discrimination ... in reaction to the war on terror, increased domestic surveillance, and the Patriot Act, many American Muslim individuals also began to view their own government as discriminatory. Many American Muslim individuals...[and groups] ... protest and ... [seek to] ... change what they see as

---

[55] O. Moyd, *Redemption in Black Theology* (Valley Forge, PA: Judson Press, 1979), 180.

[56] See J. Craven, "Malcolm X Told Us Everything We Need to Know about Donald Trump's Meetings With Black Celebrities," *Huffington Post.* January 29, 2017.
http://www.huffingtonpost.com/entry/malcolm-x-donaldtrump_us_587fea11e4b00d44838 cec1e?utm_hp_ref=black-lives-matter

violations of their rights to privacy, due process, and habeas corpus. In so doing, one might argue, these persons show just how much they have become part of an old American tradition—fighting for individual rights in the face of the state's encroaching power ...[57]

Documenting reports of civil rights incidents, the council lamented that a trend appears in the reported number of "unreasonable arrests, detentions, searches/seizures, and interrogations."[58] For example, complaints concerning law enforcement techniques jumped from 7 percent of reported civil rights incidents in 2003 to 26 percent of reported civil rights incidents in 2004. At the time of this writing, the council prepares to protect constituents from the trend in hate crimes against Muslims since the inauguration of the current U.S. president. The council hopes that American law enforcement will be able to arrest the national mind's infection of racism and anti-Muslim rhetoric.[59]

Schoeninger: Not only were Mrs. Tallis and her daughter African-American and Muslim, they were also female. And the police who traumatized them were male. She appears to come at the undercover police forcefully to protect her children. Do you believe they misunderstood her intentions and reacted out of fear?

Zeiders: Quite possibly. A lioness protecting her cubs could frighten anyone. Stamper asserts that:

> A scared cop overcompensates, which means he or she is likely to come across as loud, abrasive, arrogant. And mean—a bully. And that leads to an inescapable conclusion: scared cops are a

---

[57] Council on American-Islamic Relations,, "The Status of Muslim Civil Rights in the United States," in E. Curtis, ed., The Columbia Sourcebook of Muslims in the United States (New York: Columbia University Press, 2008), 268.

[58] CAIR, Status, 269.

[59] For updates, see Council on American-Islamic Relations' website at https://www.cair.com

danger—to themselves, and to the people they've been hired to protect and serve ...[60]

Schoeninger: Motivated to protect her children, Mrs. Tallis expressed aggressive energy toward the undercover male police wearing hoodies. In the event that a female officer was present, would it have made a difference in the outcomes?

Zeiders: Unquestionably. A female officer would have entered the situation with the psychic expression of the female archetype. This would have caused her to intuitively grasp where Mrs. Tallis was coming from. It may be that female police officers are superior to males both administratively and on the "front lines."

> ... women supervisors, managers, and executives tend to do a better job, overall, than their male counterparts. They are more community-oriented, more inclusive, more inclined to identify and work to solve "personnel" problems, more likely to meet deadlines and produce a superior work product. They are more likely to confront bigotry, excessive force, corruption, and male officers' inattention, apathy, or worse in the face of violence against women...[61]

Schoeninger: Had a female officer been present, the police might have done things very differently. And you noted that Mrs. Tallis, the plaintiff, lost her case against law enforcement. Yet she was not personally defeated or psycho-spiritually radicalized.

Zeiders: Despite losing her legal case Mrs. Tallis won an existential spiritual point. Understanding this point vitalizes one's understanding of why her mental health is likely to improve despite the undesired outcome in court. Radicalization was never part of her process because she was grounded in her political identity at an essential level of her psyche. She disagrees with

---

[60] N. Stamper, *To Serve and Protect: How to Fix America's Police* (New York: Nation Books, 2016), 77.

[61] Stamper, *To Serve and Protect*, 225.

the police and the courts. They were wrong. They trespassed against her. Despite losing, she knows that justice was not done. This is her victory. She knows that the police and the courts came to a wrong conclusion. This knowing comes out of her sense that the establishment acted badly, that it was bad to her, and that it perverted justice.

Schoeninger: She is unlikely to stay injured because she knows she is ultimately in the right—and morally superior to the establishment which refuses to account for its trespasses against her?

Zeiders: Indeed. This knowing comes from a pristine place within her. The place of the citizen. The place to which is attributed inalienable rights. The place that is enshrined in the Declaration of Independence and protected in the Constitution. Implicit in American political psycho-spirituality is the idea that there is sanctity within the citizen and the state may not trespass against it.

Afterword
by Dale Michaels

When Jung prefaced his *Answer to Job*, he preemptively responded to parties he anticipated would, at best, dismiss his work as lacking a sufficient adherence to empiricism and science. At worst, possibly, critics would denigrate this work as unscientific and not appropriate for the canon of literature in the science of psychology.

The modern psychology was committed to the physical. The pursuit of a science of psychophysics was anchored philosophically and practically to the "*-isms*" of the modern era, with a devotion to foundations that were mechanistic, reductionist, and physical. All other ideas were often deemed inferior. This was especially true in academia, both in Europe and the United States. Through the first half of the 20th century, much of academic psychology in the States existed under the framework of behaviorism, which constricted even more severely the scope of study and discussion.

This was the context in which depth psychology existed, a pillar in psychological thought, but still peripheralized to a marked extent by academia. This was the audience Jung likely anticipated would criticize the merit of his work. He promoted the recognition of *psychic* truths, finding a place at least equal to the physical criteria so widely established as the foundation of truth, fact, and the verifiable. And he was certainly not alone and apart from some significant academicians in the earlier years of modern psychology. William James entertained a wide view of not only what could be acceptable areas of study in psychology but encouraged even more esoteric pursuits. James's scope of interests was so extensive that it may have facilitated history's adoption of a narrowed presentation of his influence. The American functionalists considered him the figurehead of their movement, and as such, his work that was most relevant to those purposes was more prominently featured.

Jung's appeal to embrace psychic truths and the metaphysical, and James's hope that psychology would mature to include a broad range of experiences, including the spiritual, faced numerous hurdles. As mentioned, the behaviorists maintained a strict adherence to reductionist principles applied to what could be observed and for many decades were intolerant of any mentalistic constructs, to say nothing of spiritual matters. This period of behaviorist dominance was the context in which Jung introduced *Answer to Job*. In time, the cognitive school emerged to entertain more ideas within the human mind; however, spirit and faith were still not really included. And though some of the individuals within the humanistic movement embraced a more holistic approach to psychology and experience, attention to the spiritual remained in the minority of pursuits, at best. It's important to note that the humanists' influence in academia was relatively short-lived, and in a short period the cognitive movement became the dominant school in psychology, as it is today.

As psychology has historically ignored or marginalized religion and spirituality, religion and the institutions that house it have maintained a cautious approach to psychology, if not an outright rejection of the discipline. In *Psychology as Religion: The Cult of Self-Worship*, Paul Vitz provides the discussion that posits modern psychology as a problem for the individual and essentially society. Certain notions such as self-actualization can seem incompatible with religious teachings, especially as we transition to a postmodern psychology whereby knowing an absolute truth is questionable at best.

The real influence of academic psychology upon the individual within society is variable, however, and in the clinical domain that influence is relevant in the training of practitioners, helpers, and healers. And, it is certainly relevant to those who suffer and are looking for help and healing. Modern clinical psychologists may tend to look at the religious/spiritual dimensions of the person in front of them as irrelevant or even pathological. At best, many adherents to cognitive approaches may look at belief and faith as simply cognitions that may be included in an inventory among many other beliefs and thinking. These beliefs may be viewed as part of that person's learning and history of experience, but the interpersonal or transpersonal dimensions will be ignored. This ignoring is not necessarily intentionally dismissive but reveals a lack of experience addressing those aspects of the human being. Thus, the religious/spiritual may be viewed as irrelevant within the context of competing cognitions with which the clinician is more interested and more familiar. Furthermore, an individual who focuses on religious/spiritual images, ideas, and thoughts risks being pathologized by a practitioner in this climate that is both secular and prone to diagnostic metrics.

Here is where Zeiders's present work finds its crucial home. The clinician who aspires to treat the individual wholly and respect, attend to, and thoughtfully incorporate the religious/spiritual dimension has a limited body of literature from which to draw both information and inspiration. There needs to be a choreography between secular psychology and the religious/spiritual. Zeiders's thoughtful attention to those two domains—a clinical psychology informed by foundational education and practice, and a personal attunement to the meaningfulness of religion and spirituality—provides a template for practice.

The feature of the forensic evaluator is noteworthy. Here we have a process, an individual's history, and the need for a remarkably compressed conceptualization of a case. The evaluation is critical as a nexus for decisions—analyzing past, present, and future, and embracing both a therapeutic mindset and a legal one. There is a challenge to know the whole person, and including the religious and spiritual adds complexity and, in some ways, depth to the analysis. However, it is apparent that the individuals in these cases could not be known wholly without attention to their religious/spiritual selves. Their faith is an organizing principle within them and a tether to something so meaningful outside of them—to their community and God—that to ignore it would be missing key internal *and* external resources. As Zeiders notes, there is support for the strength of faith and the church—pastor, home groups, Sunday school, and worship, people that pay attention to this part of the person and their experience—as psychological resources. These are some of the provisions supporting the health-positive benefits of organized religion to which Zeiders refers.

There are many lessons in this work, too many to enumerate. The ethics of practice, the relevance of religious involvement to interpretation of narrative, and responses on psychological measures ... The fulfillment of bridging secular psychology to religious/spiritual individuals is at the core of this work. The world has become more complex, and we've been exposed to a diversity of beliefs, both secular and religious, from around the world. There are, however, foundational beliefs and truths that are relevant through time and space, and religious symbols that have endured. The depth psychology presented by Zeiders attends to this realm of diversity, and in the continuum from conscious experience to the unconscious. As he reminds us, there is a vantage point of depth psychology—the expert's role is organized in the servant's role. This archetypal servant, here the forensic psychologist, is a fulfillment of both Jung and James. There is a commitment to objective truth and psychological truth, and it is supported by a body of work that recognizes the influence of science, faith, and organized religion.

Zeiders notes that he is drawn to cases in which he can tell the truth and provide a blessing:

> Even in gravely legal matters, telling the truth and providing blessings is a way—while remaining professionally appropriate—to be of some service to God and man, and hopefully imitate Christ.

In a recent discussion I had with the author, he highlighted a wish fulfillment, wanting the individuals with whom he works to receive more than he suspects in their contacts within the clinical world, and even from their legal proceedings. Given the scarcity of educational institutions and opportunities to provide clinicians the foundation to meet individuals with an attunement to their religious/spiritual selves, it is a fair assumption that these people have not been treated wholly. This means their religious/spiritual selves have not been validated by the professional world that holds much of their fate in its hands—both psychological and practical. These core parts, these organizing parts, are left out of evaluation, interpretation, and thus left out of treatment. This book is thus a template for maintaining a faithful and ethical commitment to the profession, and a commitment to the whole person and their faith, as well as the community, the church, and God.

I would be remiss if I did not also reflect on a noteworthy theme within the work—the attention to trauma. Beyond the clinical symptomatology, trauma anchors a person to the past by means of persistently maintaining the psychological experience of trauma in the "now." The individual drags the experience and memory along, and it is ever-present. The mind and body respond to the world in a manner primed by traumatic experiencing so that the anticipation of threat distorts the present, and markedly influences and diminishes the expected future. The clinician certainly plays a role in what the present book frames as the refurbished future.

Sandra Bloom's Sanctuary Model establishes "future" as part of the shared language essential to conceptualizing and responding to trauma. The need to attend to the future is many-layered. The neurobiology of trauma contributes to the aforementioned anchor to the past, as the brain adapts to respond to the psychologically intolerable. The response system, always at the ready to maintain the individual's psychological integrity in the face of trauma and adversity, becomes more easily dysregulated by circumstances that cue or trigger emotions and memory that lie below the conscious, rational self. Often, there is too much attention and energy directed or reserved for the present to allow the mind to contemplate a future, to create a fantasy. Others are so shaped by a past of complex and persistent adversity that a different future is virtually nonsensical. Another part of that shared language is safety. It is possible that the religious and spiritual realm of the transpersonal may be the only means by which some individuals may transcend their earthbound trauma and reestablish meaning in a life where faith provides a safe haven for regaining a sense of a different future.

Zeiders shines a light on an essential psychic truth—the attention to faith is indispensable for the suffering individual, and therefore the clinicians to which they turn for help and healing. If the postmodern clinician is to treat the whole person, then this book demonstrates the deep connections one's faith has to a human history woven into religious writings and symbols, as well as a metaphysical world in which that psyche exists. And, the relationships maintained with that spiritual self are remarkably critical to healing, as the spiritual community provides a place of interpersonal and transpersonal experience where a shared sense of understanding of self and the world is comforting and sustaining. It should be our hope that a clinician, as exemplified in *Faith, Forensics, and Firearms*, may attend to that spiritual self and fulfill the pursuit of treating the whole person.

Acknowledgments

Special thanks to the three plaintiffs and their attorneys who gave permission to share their stories. Your plight is true and thus invaluable. Acknowledgment to Arnie Kotler. Your editing and representation have made the difference. To Sam Knapp, revered ethicist of the Pennsylvania Psychological Association, who guided me in "blinding" the reports while keeping clinical integrity. Gratitude to the *Journal of Christian Healing* for permission to republish articles as chapters. Special thanks to Robin Caccese for her diligent edits and encouragement. Great thanks to the Association of Christian Therapists and the International Association for Jungian Studies for opening their rare resources on human nature to my scholarly eyes hungry for understanding. And sincere thanks to Chiron Publications for their professionalism and swiftness bringing this book to print.

Endless thanks to Emily Selvin and Sebastian Dion for their love and support while I perspired over manuscripts and looked everywhere for grace.

About the Author

Charles Zeiders, PsyD is a clinical and forensic psychologist practicing in the greater Philadelphia area. An expert in the psychology of religion and psychological assessment, he is clinical director of Christian Counseling and Therapy Associates of the Main Line in Havertown, Pennsylvania, and holds privileges in the Department of Psychiatry at Bryn Mawr Hospital of the Main Line Health System. A postdoctoral fellow of the University of Pennsylvania's Center for Cognitive Therapy, Dr. Zeiders is emeritus chair of the Psychotherapist Specialty Group of the Association of Christian Therapists (now ACTheals).

He is a diplomate in cognitive behavioral therapy and a certified cognitive forensic therapist (National Association of Cognitive-Behavioral Therapists), among the few Ivy League-trained clinicians who unify cognitive-behavioral therapy, Jungian psychology, and integrative mental health. He teaches at Eastern University and Reformed Episcopal Seminary, and is author of *The Clinical Christ: Scientific and Spiritual Reflections on the Transformative Psychology Called Christian Holism* and other publications, available at drzeiders.com. Correspondence may be sent to drzeiders@drzeiders.com.

About the Contributors

Douglas Schoeninger, PhD earned his doctorate in clinical psychology at the University of Wisconsin, having studied with Dr. Carl Rogers. He taught at the University of North Carolina, Chapel Hill. He worked on a project facilitating Christian workers living out their faiths in their places of employment (Metropolitan Associates of Philadelphia) and was then employed at Eastern Pennsylvania Psychiatric Institute (EPPI) in Family Psychiatry. At EPPI, he received training in contextual family therapy from Drs. Ivan Nagy, Margaret Cotroneo, and Barbara Krasner, and worked with Drs. Cotroneo and Krasner on integrating spirituality and psychotherapy and healing of relationships. He is a past president of the Association of Christian Therapists (ACTHeals) and is the editor of ACTHeals' *Journal of Christian Healing*. Dr. Schoeninger has practiced individual, couples, and family therapy for many years. He is committed to applying the insights of generational healing in families to healing wounded history in organizations, communities, institutions, and nations. He is the coauthor with Judith Shelly, DMin, of *Healing Generational Wounds*.

Dale Michaels, MS, LPC is associate professor of psychology and on the faculty in the Master's in Community and Trauma Counseling at Thomas Jefferson University in Philadelphia. He is a licensed professional counselor with over 30 years of experience in residential treatment and private practice working with children, adolescents, and adults. He received his bachelor's degree from Messiah College and completed his graduate work at Villanova University.

Sources

With thanks to the *Journal of Christian Healing* and editor Douglas Schoeninger, PhD for permission to adapt the following articles into the chapters of this book.

Chapter 1 – Faith, Forensics, and Firearms
Originally published as "Faith, Forensics, and Firearms: A Case Study with Discussion of Professional and Spiritual Considerations for Forensic Experts of Faith," in *Journal of Christian Healing* (Vol. 31, No. 2), Fall/Winter 2015.

Chapter 2 – A Plight Like Job's
Originally published as "A Forensic Case of Mental Devastation from Trauma, Grief and Betrayal with Jungian, Spiritual and Cognitive-Behavioral Discussion," in *Journal of Christian Healing* (Vol. 32, No. 2), Fall/Winter 2016.

Chapter 3 – The Citizen Who Sued the Police and the Political Spiritualties of Otherness
Originally published as "The Case of the Citizen who Sued the Police and The Political Spirituality of 'Otherness,'" in *Journal of Christian Healing* (Vol. 33, No. 2), Fall/Winter 2017.